THE PASTORAL CARE
OF FAMILIES

THE PASTORAL CARE
OF FAMILIES

ITS THEOLOGY AND PRACTICE

William E. Hulme

WITHDRAWN
by Unity Library

UNITY SCHOOL LIBRARY
Unity Village
Lee's Summit, Missouri 64063

ABINGDON PRESS
New York • Nashville

THE PASTORAL CARE OF FAMILIES
ITS THEOLOGY AND PRACTICE

Copyright © 1962 by Abingdon Press

All rights in this book are reserved.
No part of the book may be reproduced in any
manner whatsoever without written permission of
the publishers except brief quotations embodied in
critical articles or reviews. For information address
Abingdon Press, Nashville 2, Tennessee.

Library of Congress Catalog Card Number: 61-11784

Scripture quotations unless otherwise noted are from the
Revised Standard Version of the Bible and are copyright
1946 and 1952 by the Division of Christian Education of
the National Council of the Churches of Christ in the
U.S.A.

MANUFACTURED IN U. S. A.

DEDICATION

TO MY
MOTHER AND FATHER
WITH MUCH GRATITUDE

Contents

chapter I

PASTORAL THEOLOGY

Each area of pastoral care from the ministry to older people to pastoral counseling with alcoholics has become a specialized ministry with its own specialized source book. In the face of this increasing specialization in the pastoral ministry there is a growing need to see the whole rather than merely the parts. Even as the minister must preach and teach, so also must he do pastoral work. He needs a guide that should to some extent cover the field, leaving him the opportunity to follow up his interests in any specific field of concentration.

But even in a book that purports to cover the field some limitation is needed to preserve a sense of unity in this rapidly expanding and diversified area. I have chosen for this unifying limitation the epochs in the human life story—those stages in the common life as it centers around family life. This is not a family-centeredness in the sense of contemporary "familism," as exampled in the host of television family series, some better, some worse, but all of them overly sentimentalized, or in certain family-centered ministries and church programs that make the single person feel out of place. Rather the emphasis is family-centered in the sense that all of us are more or less participants in the family experience. Most people have grown up in some sort of family experience. Most people have some present contact with their families.

There is another reason why this particular limitation has been chosen. Our present day is characterized by family instability. We are confronted with this both in terms of poor marital relationships and of delinquent children. The awareness of a marriage and family break down in our society is an old story, but youth on the rampage is a post World War II phenomenon. Community after community has been gripped by the terror of adolescent barbarity and has been frustrated in combating it.

These common life experiences have a specific religious significance. Marriage and family are orders of creation, while childhood, adolescence, middle life and old-age are stages in the development of the human being. Not only are these epochs vital areas in creation: God as Creator is also God as Redeemer, and redemption means the redemption of creation, its orders and its persons. Consequently these common life experiences are the objects of pastoral concern, and if pastoral theology is going to concentrate anywhere, it must concentrate here.

Pastoral Role Unique

The rise of pastoral interest in the problems of marriage and family stems in part from the rise of other professions dealing with these same problems. The family case worker, clinical psychologist, marriage counselor, geriatrics worker, and psychiatrist are all involved in the same areas of concern. Where these professions are available as community services, they are a great help to the pastor. He looks upon them as members of a team to which he also belongs and with whom he can cooperate in terms of referral and consultation. As a minister of the gospel, the pastor is a distinct member of this team and not an overlapping member. His is a ministry of the living Word of God as it centers in the Scripture and sacraments in the setting of the Church. His pastoral challenge is to help people discover in a meaningful way the application of this Word to these common life experiences and crises.

In our day the pastor has been greatly helped in this challenge by the personality and social sciences whose data have enlarged our understanding of the Word as it applies to these epochs. Some have found it difficult to relate the data of science to that of revelation on the basis that science is the word of man while revelation is the Word of God. Although these descriptions have their value in helping us to keep our thinking straight regarding the unique character of the Christian message, the realm of nature (science) and the realm of grace (revelation) are integrated in the life of the believer by the perspective of his own Christian experience. For this reason we are living in a time that gives fresh opportunity for the application of the Christian faith to the common life. In the words of Canon Wedel, "It is only in our present age of biblical rediscoveries that the personal symbols of our Bible have a chance to be fully revived. Modern psychology and sociology can be great aids in this crucial task." [1]

The very advantage that the sciences offer to pastoral care presents it with its greatest danger. Instead of having theology made more relevant by sociological insights, we may end up with sociology plus a dash of religion. It is one thing to be a pastoral theologian who is alert to psychological insights; it is another to be simply a pastoral psychologist. The initial stage of adjusting to the new insights is about over. The pastoral ministry has opened itself up to receive what the personality sciences have to offer. The challenge before us now is to incorporate these insights of science into a fundamentally theological motif. The fact that these insights are the product of the word of man, science, or that they have been used by humanists and atheists in the other professions in line with their own point of view, does not determine their value to the ministry. Rather their value is determined

[1] *The Interpreter's Bible* (Nashville: Abingdon Press, 1953), X, 728.

by the degree to which the pastor has oriented them to a dominantly theological perspective. The danger that confronts us now is that the pastoral ministry may lose its distinctive character by developing a psychological rather than a theological motif. Nor is the answer in finding some sort of a synthesis of the two, so that when psychological meets theological, some new product is the result. Only the incorporation of the new in terms of an expansion of the same basically theological function will meet the challenge.

Functions of the Pastoral Ministry

The pastoral ministry is carried out through the functions of pastoral counseling, pastoral visitation, preaching, teaching and organization. All of these are united by the fundamental motif of communicating the Gospel, but each has its own distinct way of doing so. Preaching is proclaiming. Although other purposes are involved, the aim of preaching is to inspire the hearer into a dialogue with God, the outcome of which is action in the name of God—obedience, praise, surrender, sacrifice, reception, trust. Teaching centers in clarity of understanding. Although the whole man is involved in the dynamics of teaching, the emphasis is on intellectual comprehension. Emotional insights may accompany the learning process, but the route is through the process of explaining.

Pastoral counseling centers in problem solving. It is a relationship-centered function in which the person and his problem occupy the point of focus. In contrast to preaching and teaching the communication of the Gospel in pastoral counseling is as much nonverbal as verbal, and centers in discovery as this takes place within the dynamic of interpersonal relating. Pastoral visitation means pastoral entry into the homes and lives of people. Here the initiative is with the pastor as he seeks out the sheep. In having this entry by virtue of his profession, the pastor has an opportunity to take the initiative which none of the other members of the team has. It is unfortunate that this privilege is being surrendered more and more to the stewardship and evangelism departments of church life at the expense of the department of pastoral services. Once again the pastoral ministry needs to take the initiative and not only reassert its historic privilege but make use of it. When the pastor calls on his people, his very presence as pastor brings in the gospel as background if not foreground. For this reason visitational conversation in and of itself is an *unobvious* communication of the gospel—what Luther called, "the Word in Christian conversation"—and may lead to pastoral counseling or even teaching. Organization deals with efficiency of operation. It consists in organizing the resources and means available within the scope of the Church and community for the pastoral ministry.

The personality and social sciences have been helpful also in making more effective these media of communication. This has been especially true of pastoral counseling, where the insights from the fields of dynamic psychology and clinical psychology have all but revolutionized the pastoral approach to people with problems. It is certainly true also of teaching. The results of all the scientific investigation of the teaching and learning processes in addition to what we have learned about group dynamics have been available to the religious education department of our churches. The study of homiletics has profited greatly by the help we have received from the sciences in understanding the recipient of the sermon. The preacher is helped to apply his text to the questions people are asking and not simply to questions he thinks they *should* be asking. In other words he relates his message to where people are already listening.

Pastoral visitation has profited by the emphases of the

sciences that the visitor should listen as well as speak, and try to understand as well as to be understood. This approach opens visitation to the possibilities of real sharing. The pastor as an organizer is realizing as never before the potentialities of more effective ways and techniques—*gimmicks* if you will —for working with individuals and groups within the church framework. In many cases this has meant a revitalizing of existing church groups for pastoral purposes as well as the creation of new channels for carrying out the pastoral ministry. For some of this he is indebted to the personal and group workers of other professions.

The same challenge that exists in relating the Word to the human epochs exists also in this area of the media of communication. The pastoral ministry must retain as its basic motif in all of these media, the communication of the gospel, and at the same time utilize the valuable help that comes from the sciences in making more effective each of these media. Otherwise the pastor may fail to be a member of the team, let alone a minister of the gospel. He will end up playing simply as a second team substitute for the position that some other member in his profession can do better. In this way he lets not only his church down, but also his team.

From Deposit to Performance

Pastoral theology is a function-centered theology. It has the same basis as other branches of theology such as systematic theology, namely, the gospel, but its specific nature in contrast to such logic or reasoning-centered branches, develops out of reflection upon the function of pastoral care— the dynamic of meeting human need via the ministry of the gospel. The data from such reflection provides a deposit of theory which becomes the basis for the learning process.[2]

---

[2] For a more detailed treatment of this subject, see Seward Hiltner, *Preface to Pastoral Theology* (Nashville: Abingdon Press, 1958), pp. 15-29.

This deposit is charaterized by a theological motif in which psychological and sociological insights are incorporated. Out of this theologically oriented deposit grow the *modi operandi* and techniques of pastoral care, as they relate to the general disciplines of each medium of communication. But the growing edge of pastoral theology is this gospel-based reflection upon the function itself.

This book builds upon the assumption that the reader is acquainted with the general principles and disciplines of the major media of communication, preaching, teaching and pastoral counseling, and is interested in relating to these disciplines the deposit of pastoral theology as it centers in the epochs of family living. We shall begin with the pastoral theological deposit concerning the basis for these epochs, the epoch of marriage. From here we are led to discuss the means of pastoral care regarding both premarital guidance and marital crises. Our next epoch is the family relationship, parent and child, and the pastoral theological deposit associated with it. We shall go out from this to the communication of this deposit to parents and children in terms of pastoral care. Following this we shall turn to the epoch of increasing importance, youth, and deal first with our pastoral theological understanding of this stage of development and go out from here to the actual ministry to youth. Our next epoch is middle life, first our theological approach and then our pastoral care. From here we enter into the stage of life of increasing importance in our society, namely, old age, and view it from its religious perspective and from this develop our pastoral approach. There is still much work to be done before a fully developed pastoral theology emerges. At every stage in the life cycle of the family, however, we shall find important insights coming from our theological reflection, which will help us set our pastoral care in a larger perspective.

chapter II

A THEOLOGICAL APPROACH
TO MARRIAGE

Premarital counseling and marital counseling sound alike but this is about all they have in common. Premarital counseling is functionally misnamed, since normally it is not counseling but guidance. Marital counseling is by and large counseling in the accurate sense of the word. Though functionally different, premarital guidance and marital counseling as they center in the office of the ministry are both related in one way or another to a growing body of knowledge that for want of a better name we can call a Christian approach to marriage. It is growing because the increase in the premarital and marital counseling activities among the clergy has stimulated much pastoral reflection on this subject. Premarital guidance is also growing because of the increasing amount of research data concerning marriage that is being made available through the social sciences. This data has done much to amplify the ideas in the biblical teachings about marriage. We shall begin with these biblical teachings as a base for the Christian approach to marriage and develop the ideas in terms of the insights from the pastoral ministry and the clarifying data from the social sciences.

Christ and His Church

The words of institution for marriage came out of the creation story of Genesis. "Therefore a man leaves father and mother and cleaves to his wife, and they become one flesh."

Here is the Creator's will for progress. The new must supplant the old. For the *cause* one must leave in order to cleave, and this means a radical change. There is a natural resistance to this change due to the inertia of human nature, and out of this resistance come difficulties. Newlyweds find it hard to make this break. Even though it may be made geographically, it may not be made psychologically. When this occurs hey leave by bringing along patterns of the old that are translated into the new, but basically nothing has changed. The new wine has been put into old wineskins, and it will not work for a marriage any more than for wine.

If children find it hard to leave father and mother, parents find it just as difficult to let them leave. The dependency that characterizes the relationship of children to their parents can reverse itself. The needs which the child fills in the parent's life may go unfulfilled if the child leaves. This the parent may subconsciously resist. In addition there is a natural time lag in adjusting to a change of roles. If the parent has been thinking of the child as a child throughout his years of growing up, he is not suddenly going to think of his child as an adult simply because of the wedding ceremony. The necessary shift in viewpoint that this requires may not come without a resort here or there to the use of force. So there is a mutual pull on the part of both the newlyweds and their parents against the change demanded by the new relationship. But the break with the old must be made in order to establish the new role. Before the new pattern of marriage becomes a union, a clear-cut perception of differentiating old and new loyalties is necessary.

The union of one flesh in marriage is illustrated by the relationship of God to his people in both the Old and New Testaments. In the Old Testament it is the familiar figure of Jahweh's relationship with Israel. In Hosea we read, "And in that day, says the Lord, you will call me, 'My Husband'." From Isaiah, "For your Maker is your husband." And again,

"As the bridegroom rejoices over the bride, so shall your God rejoice over you." From Jeremiah, "Surely as a faithless wife leaves her husband, so have you been faithless to me, O house of Israel, says the Lord."

The New Testament writers interpret the analogy as indicative of the relationship between Christ and the Church and expand it to an even fuller extent. Jesus himself is responsible for this in his reply to the Pharisees concerning why his disciples contrasted to those of John the Baptist did not fast. "Can the wedding guests fast while the bridegroom is with them?" Paul directly identifies the bride with the Church when he told the Corinthians, "I betrothed you to Christ to present you as a pure bride to her one husband." It is in the book of Revelation that the familiar figure of the Church as the bride adorned for her husband is put into its eschatological setting in terms of the new Jerusalem. "Come, I will show you the Bride, the wife of the Lamb. And in the Spirit he carried me to a great high mountain, and showed me the holy city Jerusalem coming down out of heaven from God."

The biblical figure serves as a two-way contact between the ordinary common life of human beings and the mysteries of God. On the one hand the familiar relationship of marriage provides a meaningful mental image by which the human being can grasp the intimacy as well as the binding tie in the relationship of God to his people. On the other hand the idea that Christ and his Church form a marriage relationship presents an example of the marital ties after which human marriages should pattern themselves. It is this latter meaning that is brought out and developed in the letter to the Ephesians, where the relationship of Christ to his Church gives structure not only to marriage but to all human relationships, even in such fields as the economic world of management and labor. Calvin sums up this two-way contact between human ordinances and the mysteries of God in his comment on this Ephesian figure.

He (the writer) proceeds to enforce the obligations of marriage by representing to us Christ and his Church; for a more powerful example could not have been adduced. The strong affection which a husband ought to cherish towards his wife is exemplified by Christ, and an instance of that unity which belongs to marriage is declared to exist between himself and the Church. This is a remarkable passage on the mysterious intercourse which we have in Christ.[1]

The analogy to marriage in Ephesians is most famous for its dictum that the union of marriage is structured with the husband as the head of the wife.

Be subject to one another out of reverence for Christ. Wives be subject to your husbands, as to the Lord. For the husband is the head of the wife as Christ is the head of the church, his body, and is himself its Savior. As the church is subject to Christ, so let wives also be subject in everything to their husbands. Husbands, love your wives as Christ loved the church and gave himself up for her, that he might sanctify her, having cleansed her by the washing of water with the word, that the church might be presented before him in splendor, without spot or wrinkle or any such thing, that she might be holy and without blemish. Even so husbands should love their wives as their own bodies. He who loves his wife loves himself. For no man ever hates his own flesh, but nourishes and cherishes it, as Christ does the church, because we are members of his body. "For this reason a man shall leave his father and mother and be joined to his wife, and the two shall become one." This is a great mystery, and I take it to mean Christ and the church; however, let each one of you love his wife as himself, and let the wife see that she respects her husband. (Eph. 5:21-33)

[1] *Calvin's Commentaries*, The Epistles of Paul to the Galatians and Ephesians (Grand Rapids, Mich.: Eerdmans Publishing Co. 1958) p. 323.

In a former day this idea of the headship of the husband was resisted by women and gloried in by men. Now it is resisted by men and gloried in by women.

The idea obviously has some background in the patriarchal society of Israel, and in this respect must adjust itself to our modern democratic society with its emphasis on the equality of the sexes (still more of an ideal than a reality). The basics in biblical thought must find their several expressions in terms of the uniqueness of every culture. Obviously in our society the cruder forms of a wife's subservience to her husband are blacklisted from the start. But if the whole of the Ephesian letter is taken seriously, we can see that these crudities were blacklisted from the beginning. The entire section on marriage is set against the background of the introductory sentence, "Be subject to one another out of reverence for Christ." Any subservience of wife to husband comes out of a mutual subservience—including that of husband to wife—out of respect for Christ. Here is a democratic ideal with a reverse emphasis from our own. While we tend to define our democracy as a society where I am as worthwhile as anybody else, in this Ephesian concept it is a society where everybody else is as worthwhile as I. In fact with its mutual subservience idea it is a society where in lowliness of mind each esteems the other better than himself. The key to the difference is the phrase, "out of reverence for Christ."

The character of Christ is also the key to the difference between the common idea of what it meant by the husband as head of the wife and the biblical idea. The biblical idea is patterned after a most unusual head. Instead of having others wash his feet, as any other master would have done, Jesus washed the feet of his disciples. Instead of desiring to be served as a Lord, he desired to serve as a servant. This subservience of the Lord to his followers has been taken into the Christology of the Church by Paul in his familiar Philippian passage,

Have this mind among yourselves, which you have in Christ Jesus, who, though he was in the form of God, did not count equality with God a thing to be grasped, but emptied himself, taking the form of a servant, being born in the likeness of men. And being found in human form he humbled himself and became obedient unto death, even death on a cross. (Phil. 2:5-8.)

Behind this New Testament observation is the Old Testament portrait of the Suffering Servant.

Who hath believed our report? and to whom is the arm of the Lord revealed? For he shall grow up before him as a tender plant, and as a root out of a dry ground: he hath no form or comeliness; and when we see him, there is no beauty that we should desire him. (Isa. 53:1-2.)

Who hath believed our report? Jesus knew how hard it is for human beings to comprehend the unusual nature of Messianic headship. To his disciples he said,

The kings of the Gentiles exercise lordship over them; and those in authority over them are called benefactors. But not so with you; rather let the greatest among you become as the youngest, and the leader as one who serves. For which is the greater, one who sits at table, or one who serves? Is it not the one who sits at table? But I am among you as one who serves. (Luke 22:25-27.)

Messianic headship is the opposite of all natural (Gentile) status consciousness and demanding of rights due to position. Yet in spite of the clarity of the Bible on this unique meaning of headship, we still interpret the idea of head in the Gentile way. We reject the biblical pattern of headship in marital life because we think it reflects only Israel's patriarchal society to which the writer of the Esphesian letter does not refer at all; and we overlook the background of Israel's Messiah, to which the writer appeals directly as his source of authority.

The head to which Ephesians refers loves his wife as Christ loved the Church. Those who see an injustice to womanhood in this structure need to meditate on this. How did Christ love the Church? He cleaves her to himself by "giving himself up for her." It is this self-sacrifice on the part of Christ that ties the Church to him. We respond to what has been given to us. It is this that ties the wife to her husband. She responds to what has been given to her. The Church father, Chrysostom, whose society was far less concerned about woman's rights than ours, took pains to bring this point home to the men of his congregation in his famous sermon on this text.

In the same way then as He (Christ) laid at His feet her (His people) who turned her back on Him, who hated, and spurned and disdained Him, not by menaces, nor by violence, nor by terror, nor by anything else of the kind, but by his unwearied affection; so also do thou behave thyself towards thy wife . . . 'But what,' one may say, 'if a wife reverence me not?' Never mind, thou art to love, fulfill thine own duty.[2]

"Even so husbands should love their wives as their own bodies." The wife is the husband's own body following the analogy that the Church is Christ's own body. Probably the original idea comes from the Genesis story of the institution of marriage when Adam, unable to find any helper fit for him among the beast of the field, found it in the woman who was made from his own rib. "This at least is bone of my bones and flesh of my flesh; she shall be called Woman because she was taken out of Man." (Gen. 2:23.) The Pauline analogy

[2] Chrysostom "Homily XX," *Library of the Fathers* (London: Oxford Press, 1860) , V, 315, 322.

of the Church as the body of Christ takes on the old bridal imagery of God to his people, which could well be its origin. If it is so then the Church is the body of Christ because she is the bride of Christ, and the wife as the husband's own body would have its basis in the very nature of marriage as it is constituted in its biblical institution.

But the husband does more as head than loving his wife, although this is the basis for everything else. He is head of the wife in terms of responsibility before God for the marriage. He assumes the responsibility for the direction of family living. His is a leadership that the wife helps him to accept by showing him respect. Exponents of modern democracy may prematurely reject this leadership role for the husband. As products of our culture we can become so bound by it that we cannot look objectively at anything that seems to run counter to its thought forms. Our social sciences can help us in our interpretation of these biblical concepts. For example the apparently crude statement that woman ought not to speak in the church has as its *raison d'être* the prevention of woman usurping authority over the man. Although the first and second centuries had different manifestations of such usurping than the twentieth, our modern resistance to seeing any wisdom behind these precautions may prove costly to our society. The abusive tyrant who once may have "ruled the roost" in a distorted idea of what being the head of the home meant, is gone, and we are now in danger of the opposite condition. We have gone from too much man in the home to no man. This is the unexpected boomerang of woman suffrage. Woman became equal by becoming manlike. In this usurpation of the male role the woman may have thought she was going from the less important to the more important role. Actually it is not a question of importance at all, but of a difference in function. From the point of view of the social sciences both roles are needed not only for a balance in society but for the development of each other. Now that men have largely been deposed as heads, they have grown to like the lack of responsibility for the marriage and the family. Women on the other hand are liking their leadership role less and less and want their men to rise up and take hold—and be men. In other words they want to give them respect. But it is now the men who are resisting.

We are realizing more today than we have for a long time that real suffrage for women is equality of a woman in being a woman. The head is not alone. There is also the body. If man is the head, woman is the heart. Here is a femininity designed by the Creator to complement masculinity. The heart responds to the head as the Church responds to Christ, and in responding makes tangible to the world the person of Christ. The woman gives the feeling tone to the home. She creates its atmosphere. As one teen-ager who had recently lost his mother by death said, "Don't get me wrong. I love my Dad. But when the mother is gone out of the home, there just isn't any home left." Here is the heart of the home in the biblical sense of the word—the seat of the warmth and tenderness. It is summed up in one aspect in the human response to the word "mother," and in another in the man's reaction to the word "wife." It is that something that goes with femininity in the home setting. I have been home alone at times when my children return home from school. One by one the door opens with the enthusiastic call, "Hey, Mom!" It was this "Hey, Mom!" that moved one mother whom I know to quit her job. "I realized not only what I myself was missing but what I was failing to give my children by not being *there.*"

Even as the husband needs his wife's encouragement to assume his role, so also the wife needs her husband's encouragement to value her role. The career of homemaker needs greater prestige in our society. The husband is the person who can raise this prestige by giving recognition to his wife's accomplishments. She is very likely to value her role as she feels her husband values it. However, it is one thing to value it and another to patronize. There is the minister for example who as an atonement for his neglect of his marriage and family is forever publicly paying tribute to "his beloved helpmeet" who by being so faithful in the small and menial tasks of the home has made possible his giving of himself in the important and weighty matters of the world outside. What is needed is an honest appreciation and interest. He also should make it possible for her to have frequent diversions from her task and with him. From the creation story it is evident that the role of companion and the role of helpmeet go together.

The head and the heart together comprise the home. If masculinity and femininity are to be perpetuated, this family structure must stand. Each complements the other to make a balanced atmosphere in which to raise children. The two become one—as Christ and the Church—and this is mystery —a source of awe and wonder. It is not good for either husband or wife if either of them cancels out in the marriage. When one dominates the other, he destroys the stimulus he needs to fulfill his own sex. Nor is there a good effect on the children when one or other of the parents is crowded out by the other. They are confused concerning their own role as boy or girl, son or daughter, and lack the masculine and feminine balance in the home which helps them develop into manhood and womanhood. I have counseled with many young people where it was the father who had canceled out. In some cases it was the mother. The effect on the child is different than instances where father or mother is lost by death. In these cases the child usually learns to understand and accept the unbalanced home, and the unwholesome influence of an inadequate parent is missing. Also the void in the parental image may be partially filled by the memory of the departed (which is often eulogized) or by a relative or friend of the same sex who fills the gap to some extent as a parent substitute. These helps are not readily forthcoming when the loss is by divorce.

The head and heart structure is not a perfect arrangement for marriage because there are no perfect people. Like the parent-child relationship which we shall discuss in a later chapter it is a two-way street in which the initiative of either person is a stimulation to the other in fulfilling their respective roles. As with any system it is not in itself the final answer because people have to make it work. The spirit must vitalize the relationships or the structure itself will become an evil. Yet a structure is needed for marriage and it is up to us to get the best structure, and it is up to each couple to make it work. To this end they pledge themselves in the marriage vows of the Christian wedding. The wedding is the making of a covenant with each other and with God, and in this way ties in with the analogy of Christ and his Church who also are covenanted together with the sacrament of baptism as the covenant or marital seal. It is this covenanted loyalty that gives to love its endurance, enabling it to go beyond the up-and-downness of romantic love without denying romantic love its full place.

The Sanctity of Sex

The sexual relationship of marriage is the symbol and the expression of two becoming one in the covenant of marriage. When we look at marriage against the background of the union between Christ and his Church, the religious significance extends also to the sex act. Its sacramental nature comes out when we realize that the physical act is actually the mediator for the total expression of union between husband and wife, even to the deepest spiritual dimensions of this union. Seen in this total concept of marriage and its involvements, the choice of marriage as a human analogy for the covenant between God and his people is a bold symbol indeed.

The sexual relationship is the unique means by which husband and wife express their covenanted relationship of love with each other and join the Creator in the process of new life. This idea of sex has always been difficult for humanity to accept. People either consign sex solely to the area of biology and abandon themselves to it for whatever biological gratification they can get out of it, or they consign it solely to the area of biology and only with reluctance have anything to do with it or even admit its existence. The latter are more likely to be religious than the former, for the religious no less than the irreligious have difficulty seeing any spiritual meaning to sex. This is largely because religious influences foreign to the religion of the Old and New Testaments have subtly permeated the Church from its beginning and distorted its witness in this whole area of the relationship of the spiritual to the physical.

The Christian Church did not enter into a religiously empty world. The Hellenist world was strongly entrenched in the religious teachings of Plato, who thought of the spiritual life in terms of pure spirit and looked upon the world of nature as at best only rungs on the ladder to lead us to the realm of God in which this transitory world of nature can never share. From the Asian east came even more extreme spiritualizing religions, teaching that the realm of nature is actually evil. Into this religious climate in which the divorce rather than the union of spirit with matter was axiomatic, came the nature-accepting Judeo-Christian movement. To expect that the Church would be uninfluenced by its own world is to expect too much. Many of the Church fathers of both the East and West unconsciously incorporated in varying degrees these nature rejecting doctrines. We see this most clearly in Augustine who on the one hand was seriously interested in the Manichaean sect which rejected the physical world as an evil, and on the other hand was indulging himself in the pleasures of sex with his mistress whom he was prevented by social distinctions from marrying. The result was an intense sense of guilt and frustration over sex which led him to Christianity and through Christianity to forgiveness and peace. But sex was a causality in the process, and Augustine was never able to incorporate it into a wholesome and spiritual frame of reference.

The trend continued until clergy were forbidden to marry and the higher morality of Roman Catholicism which espoused celibacy was firmly entrenched. In the churches of the Reformation we see the same nature-rejecting synthesis with the ancient religions in Protestant legalism and in puritan and pietistic movements which have all too often seen little connection between the realm of the spirit and sex, and have relegated its function in marriage to the procreation of the race and to the satisfaction of a biological appetite.

Even our present-day literature in the realm of Christian marriage shows the effects of this age-old distortion. The Protestant Swiss physician, Bovet, has written a widely circulated book entitled, *A Handbook to Marriage and Marriage Guidance,* which attempts to present the subject from a Christian as well as a scientific point of view. In many ways it does a commendable job, but the author consistently maintains a view of sex that is essentially Hellenistic rather than Biblical. Says Dr. Bovet:

I know dozens of married couples of all ages who by voluntary agreement have renounced the sexual side of their married life and daily place their whole life-force at God's disposal . . . It must also be added that such self-restraint in no way suggests a low evaluation of Eros. On the contrary it is only because sex is regarded as a great good that one can expect great good from sacrificing it. Anyone who is capable of surrendering this last bastion to God experiences an extraordinary feeling of freedom and is capable of breaking with every other compromise. But only when one makes the attempt does one realize how strongly one is tied to this "lawful pleasure" and how little faith one really has in absolute surrender to God. Only then can one begin to understand the real value of virginity, and how it does not necessarily mean a low estimate of the sanctity of marriage . . . Abstention by married persons as a sacrifice to God is one of the most effective answers to the ever-increasing worship of sex which affects wide circles by its power of collective suggestion. A man who has had a physical experience of how, when the living Christ wills it, this idol can fall to pieces, is in a position to proclaim a real "militant purity" . . . If abstention in marriage is an act of obedience to which one has been personally called by God, if the love previously regarded as the special prerogative of marriage is placed at his disposal, then it can be extraordinarily fruitful.[3]

While it may not necessarily mean a "low estimate of the sanctity of marriage," Bovet's position does seem to indicate a low estimate of the sanctity of the sex relationship in marriage. Putting sex into the Hellenist realm of "lawful pleasure," he separates it from its sacramental and religious significance. Granted that all too many married people do not have the right attitude toward sex, and that abstention may be needed before the right use can come about, the Christian answer is in the *right use* and not in abstention, except where conditions of health make this advisable. The God who works through nature desires to work through this natural act which He designed to bless marriage rather than through the rejection of it. Abstention is more of an insult to such a God than a sacrifice. From a purely scientific point of view Bovet has failed to recognize that the sex act is indigenous to marriage and, as it conveys the total union, is a vital contributor to the wholesome development of the marriage partners and the marriage itself. In the words of

[3] Theodore Bovet, *A Handbook to Marriage and Marriage Guidance*, pp. 65-67. By permission of Longmans, Green & Co., Ltd.

The Family Today, the Lambeth Conference Report of 1958, "Husbands and wives owe to each other and to the depth and stability of their families the duty to express in sexual intercourse, the love which they bear and mean to bear to each other." [4]

If one thinks of eros in terms of romantic or sexual love, then it is entirely within the realm of possibility that Christian agape can manifest itself also along with eros in the conjugal love of marriage. Here the kingdoms of nature (creation) and of grace (redemption) become one in Christian experience. This is the basis of the spiritual dimension to sex and the sacramental analogy of the sex act in marriage. In our day we have a great opportunity for this realization, for now more than in most former ages we can look at sex theologically without anxiety and without the compulsion to focus on precautions and prohibitions. It is also a day when we can understand the biblical figures of marriage more fully because of the helpful data of the social sciences. We are growing in our acceptance of sex as a God-given enjoyment of married love for women as well as men, even to its physical sensations.

The sacramental significance of sex in marriage is shown in the scriptural use of the word *know.* "Then Joseph being raised from sleep did as the angel of the Lord had bidden him, and took unto him his wife; and knew her not till she had brought forth her first-born son." An obviously physical act becomes an act of commitment to each other, of renewal of covenant vows, of deep relating and intimate knowing. Biology alone cannot account for this. The sex act is a symbol—and more than a symbol. It communicates that which it symbolizes. Its experience of knowing deepens with the deepening of the marriage relationship.

[4] The Report of Committee·5 of The Lambeth Conference, 1958 London, S.P.C.K. p. 8.

The Dynamics of Redemption

By its analogy of Christ and his Church the Christian approach to marriage goes beyond mere analogy and places the relationship within the dynamics of the theology of redemption. The covenant of love to which the partners pledge themselves is not only comparable to the covenant between Christ and his Church but actually receives its impetus through this covenant. Where it remains simply an analogy there is the danger that it will remain also a beautiful or even romantic ideal but hardly relevant to the kind of married life one is experiencing in the here and now. It is the actual setting of this analogy within the dynamic of redemption that takes the analogy beyond romanticism. The love between the human lovers that is an analogy of the love between Christ and his Church is not native to the lovers. The love of husband and wife not only symbolizes the love between Christ and his Church but it actually comes into being through their participation in the love between Christ and his Church. It is as they receive Christ's love as members of his body, the Church, that they themselves are enabled to give love. But the Church receives Christ's love in the medium of forgiveness. The demonstration of this love is the cross of Christ upon which he wrought the atonement for sin. The love that binds the Christian husband and wife is a love that is characterized by repentance and forgiveness, both in their relationship with God and in their relationship with each other.

Our sanctification as Christians comes through relationships. God himself relates himself to us through the redemptive love of Christ. But the divine was never meant to be a substitute for the human, nor even to be something removed from the human. God has made us to live in communion with others. In the creation story it was his observation that it was not good for man to be alone that brought about the creation of the woman and the institution of marriage. The confidence, security and initiative that move us to grow as persons come from our intimate relationships of which marriage is in the forefront. Said Chrysostom, himself an early opponent of marriage for the clergy,

> There is no relationship between man and man so close as that between man and wife, if they be joined together as they should be. And therefore a certain blessed man too, when he would express surpassing love, and was mourning for one that was dear to him, as his own soul, did not mention father, nor mother, nor child, nor brother, nor friend, but what? *Thy love,* saith he, *fell upon me as the love of women.* For indeed, in very deed, this love is of all empires the most absolute: for others may be strong, but this passion has not only strength, but unfadingness.[5]

Like God, the marital partner is both a critic and a sustainer, both a judge and an intimate helper.

Buttressing these human relationships and vitalizing them is the divine-human relationship. The religious relationship is not one among others but one in and through others—and beyond them. It is the Christian good news that we can experience this relationship even though we do not deserve it on the basis of our behavior. In the words coming out of the Reformation, we are *simul iustus et peccator,* justified simultaneously with being a sinner. This is because the relationship is established on forgiveness in which we live and move and have our being so far as our redemption is concerned. Says Calvin:

> Whom, therefore, the Lord receives into fellowship, him he is said to justify; because he cannot receive any one into favour or into fellowship with himself, without making him from a sinner to be a righteous person. This, we add, is accomplished by the remission of sins. For if they, whom the Lord has reconciled

---

[5] Chrysostom, *op. cit.,* p. 312.

to himself be judged according to their works, they will still be found actually sinners; who, notwithstanding, must be absolved and free from sin. It appears, then, that those whom God receives, are made righteous no otherwise than as they are purified by being cleansed from all their defilements by the remission of their sins; so that such a righteousness may, in one word, be denominated a remission of sins.[6]

This shows the binding power of forgiveness to hold the covenanted together. As we have seen, it initiates and sustains the relationship between Christ and his Church. It also holds in relationship the Christian husband and wife. It is this forgiveness which translates the romantic analogy of Christ and his Church to the unromantic moments of the here and now. The married partner is as perfect as the Church. Both the Church and the married partner maintain their relationship intact by living in repentance and forgiveness. The Church like the individual Christian is accepted by grace through faith, not of works lest any man should boast.

Thus it is that Christ and his Church give not only the pattern for marital relating, but the power. It is as husband and wife receive Christ's love unconditionally that each is moved to accept the other as he or she is. In this way the sanctification of the redeemed has its direct application and stimulus in family living. Here is something we can offer the world in our evangelism efforts. The nature of marriage is realized fully only in terms of the union of Christ and his Church. Therefore marriage is realized most fully, humanly speaking, among those who are united not only with each other but united with the Church of Christ. This must be said in spite of all the evidence one may procure from this or that inadequate marriage among the fellowship of the redeemed. The Church's ministry of reconciliation has a tre-

[6] John Calvin, *A Compend of the Institutes of the Christian Religion*, ed. Hugh Thomson Kerr, Jr. (Philadelphia: Presbyterian Board of Christian Education, 1939) p. 110.

mendous potential for the establishing and the healing of family ties.

Marriage from the Christian point of view is one of the units of fellowship within the great fellowship of the Church. Therefore marriage between Christians has a different center of gravity from marriages consummated outside of the dynamics of redemption. The Christian approach to marriage places the relationship of the Church to Christ at the center of the relationship of husband and wife. Nowhere is idolatry more of a danger than within the family relationships. One of the most offending statements of Jesus refers precisely to this danger. "If any one comes to me and does not hate his own father and mother and wife and children and brothers and sisters, yes, and even his own life, he cannot be my disciple." (Luke 14:26.) No human being can substitute for the place of God in one's life. When this happens, idol and idolater slowly but surely destroy each other. As one pastor tells the couples who come to him to be married, "If you expect to find in your marital partner what only Jesus Christ can give, you are going to be sadly disillusioned." It is not those who enter marriage to find the answer to their personal problems, that form genuine marriages, but those who enter marriage finding the answer to their innermost needs in Christ. It is not unto ourselves or unto our marital partner or unto anything or anyone else that is finite that we are to live, but unto him who died for us and rose again, who alone can satisfy the soul since he alone is the Infinite One. The marriage relationship grows because it goes beyond itself to the larger family of God, the Church, and as such is united with Christ.

The Problem of Birth Control

As we have seen from the biblical story of the institution of marriage two purposes for marriage are evident: the companionate helpmeet and parenthood within the medium of family living. It is in these purposes that sex finds its role in marriage. On the one hand it offers that unique expression of this union that strengthens its ties and on the other it makes possible for those so united to be quasi-partners with God in his creative activity, as our word *procreation* implies (to create *in front of,* or to bring forth).

There seems to be another purpose for sex in marriage implied in the New Testament, specifically in I Cor. 7:9: "But if they cannot exercise self-control, they should marry. For it is better to marry than to be aflame with passion." Does this not indicate that marriage exists for sex rather than sex for marriage? It would, but only if we confine our interpretation of sexual passion to Freud's troublesome biological urge—the *id* (which the Church seems prone to do). If we see it in its broader context of the total person, biology and spirit work together. Although the physical urge can become distorted through emotional disorders, it is essentially associated with a person's need to relate intimately to another. Consequently if we cease to follow the age-old error of dividing the human being into two unrelated or even antagonistic parts, body and soul, we can see that this supposed third purpose of sex is nothing more than Adam's need for intimacy, viewed from its physical side.

The role of sex in marriage can be compared to the role of food in life. Some, we say, eat to live and others live to eat. From the standpoint of reproduction, sex in marriage compares to eating to live. The sacramental role of sex in marriage would compare to eating as an enjoyable activity. There is appetite and taste to heighten the satisfaction. There is the fellowship mediated by eating together. The thanksgiving that is evoked clarified its religious significance. We could speak of this as living to eat, but actually each of these experiences is a quality of *living.* For this reason the sacramental role is still in the pattern of eating to live in the full meaning of married life as God instituted it. In neither of these functions can sex be thought of as simply dessert—nice to have but not essential for a balanced diet.

The challenge before the male and female is to integrate these two purposes of marriage, which includes fitting the two purposes of sex together. This has proved to be a source of much disturbance, as one purpose seems to work against the other. The fear of having another conception too soon or once again can destroy the purpose of sex as a communication of married love. When conception does occur under such circumstances, the parents' attitude toward the child may be anything but loving. Long after the child is born the guilt over this resentment may distort the parental relationship. Those who know the maternity wards of hospitals know the sad truth that many babies are "resigned to" rather than wanted. And as one clergyman in a church that frowns upon contraceptives said,

One of our frequent pastoral tasks is to help mothers with the anxiety they have over their babies caused by the fear that their initial resentment in having the child may bring harm to the child as a divine judgment.

But the handicap is not only on the parent; it is also on the child. Children need most of all the assurance that they are wanted.

Resentful attitudes toward pregnancy may transfer into resentful attitudes toward the cause of the pregnancy. The parent, particularly the mother, may fear and resent the sex act itself and the marital partner who shares it. This resistance to a system that sets aside human freedom may destroy something vital to married life as the Bible describes it.

The repercussions in marriage and parenthood that arise out of the difficulty in fitting together the two purposes of marriage point to the need for some type of conception control. The Old Testament implies a general control over the processes of nature in the directive from the creation narrative, "Be fruitful and multiply, and fill the earth and subdue it." The description of the world of Adam and Noah is an entirely different picture from the world of today. From a world that needed filling we have gone to a world that is in grave danger of a population explosion. The prophecies of the population of the future that mathematics can give us are simply fantastic.[7] Although mathematics do not take into account any unforeseen changes in the future, the problem is surely evident. Any attempt on the part of any group to prevent a united effort to limit conception in the overpopulated areas of poverty is open to the charge of irresponsibility. But if we base our arguments for birth control on the population explosion alone, we give the impression that Christian ethics are determined by expediency. The Christian basis for birth control was established long before the present emergency. "Be fruitful and multiply" still means that the Creator expects children to come out of marriage, and "subdue the earth" still means that man is to exercise dominion over the forces of nature. This dominion is something that lies ever before us as a challenge, as man works under his Creator in industry and research. If this is the challenge to man in the covenant of creation, how much more is it in the covenant of the *redemption* of creation, as man under God gradually increases this ability to administer the world of nature.

Despite the clarity of the creation covenant regarding man's dominion over nature, there has been a history of conflict over it. Along with the realization that nature is to be subdued, there has been the reluctance to do so because creation belongs to God. It is *his* area. If we begin to tamper with it, we may spoil it. There is something to be said for

---

[7] Richard M. Fagely, *The Population Explosion and Christian Responsibility*, (New York: Oxford University Press, 1960), also Theo. Gill, "Demographic Explosion," *Christian Century*, Aug. 6, 1958.

this fear. Whenever man attempts to subdue, he seems also to despoil. Yet does this alter the basic principle? When agriculturists produce irrigation to change the character of land where no rain has fallen, no one would accuse them of tampering with nature. Nor do we accept floods as untouchable signs of God's judgment. Rather we work on flood controls. So also with the natural realm of human reproduction. People may misuse this dominion, but this does not release us from our covenant responsibility.

In birth control the theological issue is not whether things work out any better because of conception limitation, but whether conception control is not man's responsibility under God as a part of his elevated status above all other creatures. Birth control requires a level of maturity. This is why it is often referred to as responsible parenthood. What of those who have not attained to this maturity? Are they mature enough for the greater responsibility of *being* parents? Here is the irony of the argument.

The difficulty often goes deeper than a reluctance to enter what we feel is God's area. This is indicated by the fact that this reluctance is directed primarily toward the area of human reproduction. It would seem that involved also is a latent rejection of the other purpose of sex in marriage. The ancient attitude toward sex from the Greek and Asian natural religionists has infiltrated Christian thinking more than we would like to admit. The other purpose of sex in marriage seems too sensual to have any religious validity.

In our day the question is not over whether there should be some control over conception. We can see this in the size of our families today in our urbanized and mechanized way of life in comparison to the size in the rural, horse and buggy culture of a previous day. Some couples need no limiting controls since cenception for them is such a rare occurrence that it is its own limiting factor. Some actually need professional help to achieve conception. Others need controls.

Otherwise conceptions could occur each year, and in our day of early marriage there are twenty or more such years. The controversy is obviously not over whether they should use controls, but over *what* controls they should use—whether the control is by regulating the times for intercourse as with rhythm, or by intercepting the semen during intercourse with contraceptives. How this issue will project itself into the use of the new "infertility pills" remains to be seen. From a Christian point of view the moral issue is the same in the use of contraceptives, the rhythm method, or the infertility pills. In each case the intention of the couple is to avoid conception without foregoing the marriage act, and morality centers in motivation so far as the New Testament is concerned.[8]

In spite of the lack of any moral issue in the choice of control, the controversy over the problem has resulted in a large acceptance of the rhythm method. Many make this choice for religious reasons, and some simply to avoid agitating the situation. The reasoning of those who espouse the rhythm method for religious reasons is based upon a respect for nature that identifies the natural processes with the moral law. In other words, intercepting the semen in intercourse would be contrary to what would happen in intercourse without this interception. Since the interception is a device of man's mind to prevent some of the consequences of this action of his body, it is morally wrong. From the biblical point of view this is simply bad theology. Christianity is no nature cult. We are to subdue nature, not worship it. Instead of submitting helplessly to the processes of nature, the Christian as a worker together with the Creator channels and subdues these processes to serve the purposes for which God has created and redeemed us. The birth control controversy cannot be dismissed as simply a difference over method. Behind this difference is a theological conflict over whether

[8] Paul even subjects martyrdom to this test in I Cor. 13.

there is not a higher source for the revelation of God's will than the processes of nature.

There is also the fear that contraceptives will result in less children per family. As with any of his dominions over nature, there is the danger that man will misuse contraceptives to further his own selfish end. Theoretically he can use the rhythm method in the same way. It is even possible to want children for selfish reasons, for in our day there is a growing prestige for those who have their "quiver full of them." When Father John E. Kelly of the National Catholic Welfare Conference charged that those who advocate "artificial birth control" would divide and subtract, not multiply, he is actually casting as much reflection upon the reliability of the rhythm method as he is upon the designs of contraceptive advocates.

And well he might. One of our leading gynecologists on the West Coast has openly stated that "the rhythm method is not always reliable, as fifty percent of Roman Catholic couples find out." Although Bovet goes out of his way as a theologian to see the value in the Roman Catholic position, as a physician he admits that the rhythm method even with its temperature-graph improvements is hampered by individual variations and peculiarities.[9] Once the couple's confidence is shaken in its reliability, the fear of pregnancy with all of its accompanying resentment and guilt descends ominously over the marital act.

In spite of its shortcomings for general use, the rhythm method may be the best method for some couples. For them the regularity of the woman's cycle makes for reliability and the spacing of the marital relations presents no particular problem. It is for these reasons, then, that it should be preferred, and not because it is the more God-approved method.

Behind the demand of those who for religious reasons in-

[9] Bovet, *op. cit.*

sist upon the rhythm method, there is often a cryptic admiration for abstinence. In the name of curtailing the "flesh" this admiration for abstinence is actually a concession to the "flesh." Asceticism has had a universal appeal to the religiously minded as a short cut to virtue. By using his natural human powers of discipline to prevent the satisfaction of his equally natural appetites, one develops a man-made piety which has more in common with the non-Christian religions of the East than with Christianity, and is more a feeder for pride than for love. It is a concession to the flesh because in locating the "flesh" in the body that is being disciplined, it overlooks the "flesh" in the spirit that is doing the disciplining. Discipline is needed in the marital relationship to prevent the misuse of the sex act not to prevent its use. We discipline our appetite for food so that we do not endanger the health of our body either by overeating or undereating. So also for the sex relationship for the health of the marriage. Those who appeal to the virtue of temperance as an antidote to birth control are too often grinding the ax of a crypto-asceticism. The satisfaction of an appetite is also a religious activity. Difficulties arise out of underappetite as well as overappetite. The glorification of abstinence under the guise of temperance is too easy a solution to these difficulties. It may simply be an escape from the sense of failure and from the effort to cope directly with the difficulty.

Even on the basis of its own claim to virtue—that it is in harmony with nature—the rhythm method has some serious shortcomings. Actually it runs counter to *human* nature as God created it. Eros by its very nature cannot be arbitrarily scheduled. By attempting to do so the rhythm method disregards the role of desire in the marital relationship. Sexual desire is fluctuating. It is difficult to know all of the factors that may be involved in the stimulation of desire. Physical factors are involved. Certainly mental ones are. The things that take place in a couple's day—their life together, their vocational and relaxational vicissitudes, their social and recreational experience, casual moments of affection and consideration, the natural reaction to sensory appeal, emotional ups and downs—all these and more play their role. There is reason to believe also that many women experience an increase of desire during their fertile period.[10] This is only what we would expect in a nature intelligently designed. Yet at precisely the time when husband and wife may mutually desire each other, the wife may be in her fertile period. Even affection must be curtailed, lest in fanning the flame of desire, it lead only to frustration.

The rhythm method puts an unnatural pressure on both husband and wife to restrain their desire during one phase of the cycle and just as unnatural pressure to produce those desires during the other phase. The artificiality of the arrangement runs counter to the essentially ecstatic quality of the marital union. We can scoff at romantic spontaneity only when romanticism is made the dominant motif of marriage. To eliminate its need for recognition is to disregard the role of the whole person—specifically his emotions —in sex. If nature is to be reverenced in this area, it would seem that the higher reverence should go to the distinctly human elements in this natural act, and not to the merely biological process that is common to all of the higher animals. For the anxiously inclined, the schedule of the rhythm method may make sex a more anxious ordeal than it already is. There are increasing pressures on the marital act in the speeded up tempo of our day, without adding more on the basis of bad theology. For some couples the rhythm method may satisfactorily serve the purpose, for the others it is neither reliable nor emotionally satisfying.

Those for whom the rhythm method is not satisfactory for conception control or for preserving the sacramental signifi-

[10] Bovet, op. cit., p. 88.

cance of the marriage act have an alternative in contraceptives. This method is normally regarded as the safest method of birth control. It also has the advantage of permitting intercourse when the couple desires it. By reducing the fear of pregnancy and by being adjustable so far as time is concerned, the use of contraceptives has the advantage in preserving the role of sex as an expression of married love. Although contraceptives are about as old as civilization, they have been improved and made more generally available in our modern times. May this fact have something to do with our potential today for developing more fully the total meaning and experience of marriage? The answer to this question depends upon one's theological conception of marriage. We see again that the controversy over birth control is not simply a question over method but a question of differing conceptions of marriage and of the role of sex in marriage.

There is good reason for identifying birth control with responsible parenthood. When a person takes the responsibility for conceiving a child, he is likely also to take the responsibility for preparing himself for parenthood. On the other hand when a couple take no responsibility for controlling conception, they may feel equally as irresponsible about preparing for parenthood. There is a sense of fatalism about the "act of God" that can as readily justify irresponsibility for one as for the other. Parenthood is a big undertaking and preparation for it is important even though there is much that can neither be learned nor understood until one is actually in the parenthood role.

The task of subduing nature in the institution of marriage is an activity within the realm of faith. It is part and parcel with a person's calling as a Christian and with the religious consummation of his marriage. As he takes this responsibility seriously, the obligations of parenthood sharpen into focus. The responsibility may not only seem big, but *too* big. The need for guidance is apparent. Any theological reflection upon birth control is incomplete so far as the Church is concerned until it is made relevant to the pastoral ministry. And when this is done we are quickly aware that the task of guidance goes beyond the pastor to the professional team on which the pastor belongs, which includes the physician and the marriage and family counselor.

Although the counsel of the pastor and his team members can be of great help in the making of them, these are decisions that cannot be removed for the Christian couple from the areas of the priesthood of the believer and Christian freedom. In these matters of responsible parenthood, birth controls help the couple to carry out these decisions made under God and so serve a useful purpose not in creating small families, but in creating wholesome families. The two purposes of marriage fit together. When through intelligent means the obstructive anxieties over pregnancy and guilt over its prevention are removed, the natural desire of those who share their love and life together is to have a child together. And in having a child together they are drawn by this common concern and experience to a greater intimacy and devotion to each other.

chapter III

PREMARITAL GUIDANCE

In the foregoing chapters we have surveyed the Christian approach to the marital relationship from a pastoral point of view. This body of knowledge has grown out of and relates back to the pastoral activity in the area of marriage. It has a direct relationship, therefore, to the pastor's premarital guidance. Sometimes the prospective bride or groom presents a problem to the pastor in regard to the marriage, and in these instances his premarital guidance may become premarital counseling. This awareness of a problem may even come about during the course of the premarital guidance. But for the most part young couples, even if they are aware of problems, are looking to the marriage itself as the answer to them all. The necessary disturbance that makes counseling possible is just not there.

Premarital guidance has come into its own in our recent past. Previous to the past few decades the pastor's premarital guidance was confined to the marriage ceremony itself and perhaps a wedding sermonette. But without our growing urbanization and the greater emancipation of women has come the phenomenal increase in the divorce rate. The statistics of one out of four, and then one out of three marriages ending in divorce has alarmed our society and particularly our churches. Divorce is a frightening thing, much more frightening than unhappy marriages. The burden of the responsibility seemed to point to the minister—he was the one who married them. What had he done to help them make a success of their marriage? What guidance—what information had he given them?

The minister felt the pressure. He felt it even more when

some of the marriages he himself had performed ended in divorce. What could he have done to prevent it? What could he do to prevent its happening again? It was out of this uneasiness that he developed the query approach. After assisting them in making the necessary arrangements for the rehearsal and the ceremony, he cautiously asked them if they had any questions they would like to ask him. After a moment or two of looking nonplused, the bride might think of one. "Oh, yes—there is one question—does my father walk up the aisle on my left or on my right?" Well, this is not exactly what he meant. "Do you have any questions about marriage itself?" "About marriage? No, no, none that we can think of." Now what does he do! Here they are approaching what they feel is the panacea, and he asks them if they have any questions! Besides, even if they did have a question about marriage, would they be able to ask it under these circumstances? All right, if they won't ask any questions, he will give them the answers anyhow! And so we arrive at the required lecture.

The required lecture is better than doing nothing. But it helps those most who need it least. Those most able to receive and profit from it are those who are most ready for marriage in the first place. The seeds of marital discord are implanted deeply in the personalities. They show themselves in attitudes and emotional patterns. As with any other deep-seated problem these cannot be dispensed with by an hour of advice, regardless of how fine that advice is. One obvious limitation to the lecture or to any other pattern for premarital guidance stands out—the choice of a partner has already been made. And the choice is often part of the problem.

Obviously for any thorough job of premarital guidance the pastor must begin before the couple announces to him their intention to be married. The choice of a marital partner, for example, may be conditioned by deficiencies in the personality. People usually find what they are looking for—the question is, what are they looking for? Some may be looking more for a parent than a mate, simply because they have not matured to the point where they are ready for a mate. They need someone to tell them what to do because they cannot think for themselves. Or they need someone to take care of them because by themselves they feel helpless. At the same time there are those whose immaturity is in the opposite direction. They have a need to *tell* someone what to do. Or they have a need to take care of someone—an exaggerated need to be needed. The sad truth is that these opposites have a way of attracting each other.

Others are looking for someone to boost their ego. They feel inadequate by themselves and hope to gain status through their marital choice. This same feeling of inferiority, however, can work in reverse. It can lead a person to think that he rates very little in the choice of a marital partner so that he settles for very little. In choosing very little he is also protecting himself, since now there is at least someone toward whom he can feel *superior*. Still others are looking for someone who will solve all their problems by simply loving them. They have never really known what it is to be loved, and they do not realize how unable they have become to receive it. The wounds of rejection are not easily healed. The fear continues that basically they are unlovable. For this reason even the love of the sweetheart is subjected to doubt and suspicion. Here is the psychological basis for some jealousy in marital life.

These are ways in which personality deficiencies distort the image of what we desire in a marital partner and lay the basis for marital problems. People who are extremely insecure and emotionally immature are unable either to give or to receive love. They are too self-rejecting to receive and too needy to give. Yet marriage is a sharing. They take the marriage vows and intend to follow them, but they have not the wherewithal to carry through.

If we need another reason why we must begin early with our premarital guidance program, it is the fact that a person's attitude toward sex, marriage, and the family begins early in his life. As one man who was having trouble with his marriage said, "The first time I heard about sex was in a shack where the kids of the neighborhood hung out. I couldn't imagine my parents being involved in anything like that." In his adolescence he had turned to masturbation as a solace for his loneliness and social disappointments. His shameful impression of sex caused him to feel all the more guilty over his masturbation. Out of his frustration he began to long for marriage as the answer to all of his sexual problems. In masturbation he had turned sex in upon himself as a type of self-love in which he pampered his whims and fancies. In marriage, sex is turned outward in sharing and whims have to give way to mutual desires. But when he married he simply transferred his previous attitudes toward sex to the marital union and met first frustration and then disillusion. Now he has a sex problem in marriage—but it began long before. How can the pastor meet this need to begin earlier in his premarital guidance?

The earliest place that such guidance can be given is in the home. Family attitudes are internalized by children. The girl's attitude toward men is influenced by her mother's attitude toward men. The children's attitude toward sex is shaped by the family attitude toward sex, as it is communicated to them verbally as well as non-verbally. A youth's attitude toward marriage and the family is influenced by the kind of family life he has known and by the attitudes his own parents have toward each other and the family. The conclusion is obvious—the best preparation for marriage is to have come from a happy, healthy-minded home. In saying this we are not taking into account what the grace of God can do in spite of natural handicaps. But we are recognizing that education for sex, marriage, and family is begun in the home and is meaningful only in the family context and in terms of family relationships. It is here also that personality development takes place and where mature or immature influences in what a person is looking for in a mate arise. The pastor who desires to begin early in his premarital guidance must of necessity concentrate on the home life of his people.

The organizational structure of the Church offers him an effective way of influencing this home life. Many congregations have Sunday-school classes for the parents of young children. These can also be conducted as study or forum groups meeting on a weekday. In these classes the teachings of Christianity can be taught and discussed within the perspective of family living. Special material is available for these classes at most denominational publishing houses. A small book such as *Growing Up to Love* by H. Clair Amstutz makes an excellent study guide for this group. Although the pastor may not be the teacher of the class, he is a resource person in planning and conducting the class, and through his personal and public contacts with his people, encourages their participation.

The children's Sunday-school classes offer the opportunity for a direct ministry to children. It is most important that teachers are chosen who have a healthy attitude toward the world of creation. Although the amount of time they have with the child is limited, these teachers exert a strong influence in the religious development of the child. The child may forget the specific things that a teacher says, but the attitudes in which they are spoken is not forgotten. Each teacher is also a pastor. Beside taking an active part in their selection and in their instruction, the pastor can alert these teachers to the way in which their teaching relates to long-range premarital guidance.

Most ministers do not enter into a teaching relationship with the children of the congregation until they become members of his confirmation or membership class. Here he can present the Christian picture of sex, marriage, and family in a manner commensurate with their level of comprehension. It is much better to do this within the positive implications of the doctrine of creation than within the negative context of the commandment against adultery. From both a precautionary and a pastoral point of view, it is helpful to take the parents of the children into one's confidence in these matters. Calling an occasional meeting of the parents to discuss with them what he would like to do along these lines with the children gives the pastor the opportunity to guide these parents in continuing this Christian education within the family circle. It also gives the parents the opportunity to express whatever misgivings they may have over sex education.·

His next organizational opportunity is the young people's society. We shall discuss the ministry with this group in the chapter concerning the "Pastoral Care of Youth." In his preaching ministry the pastor reaches more people directly than through any other medium. A sermon series on the Christian approach to nature, to marriage, to family living, will create considerable interest in the congregation. Here again the attitude of the preacher toward these problems of family living communicates as much as the words. When a child reaches adolescence, he needs a father confessor-confidant. Knowing this the pastor can make a special effort to make himself available for personal conferences with his youth. As he helps them overcome their familiar problems in relating to themselves and others, he is doing more for their potential as marital partners than he probably can do in any pre-marital guidance session preceding marriage.

When They Come

When an individual has profited from the advantages of such a long-range program in premarital guidance, he may not need much when he comes with his sweetheart to the minister to announce his intentions. Even though he chooses one outside the congregation—and the chances are he will—his choice reflects his background and character. This is the ideal. But the ideal and the actual can be two different things. Besides, even those best fitted for marriage can profit from some helpful guidance from the minister who marries them. So the pastor should be prepared to offer this guidance to those who ask him to perform their ceremony.

In a two-picture cartoon the first picture showed a young couple on their way to a marriage counselor for some premarital guidance. They were sitting in romantic affinity in the front seat of the automobile. The second picture showed them returning from the counselor. This time they were not even in the same seat. He was sitting with serious face at the wheel while she was in the back seat equally sober. Their eyes were opened wide. In spite of the humor there is good reason for sober discussion before marriage. What officiating clergyman has not had the experience of rejoicing in the love that unites the couple before him, only to witness this same couple at a not too distant occasion in angry charge and countercharge with apparently nothing but contempt for each other. The romantic idealism of the starry-eyed sweethearts can afford to be shaken somewhat before marriage if it means that problem areas will be seen and faced.

However, there are always those who have a neurotic fear of any new experience, particularly one that is as irrevocable and consequential as marriage. Naturally any obviously sober discussion of marriage will stir up their anxieties, and should any apprehension over going ahead with the marriage result, it may be based on anything but a realistic appraisal. Therefore, the pastor's invitation to the couple to discuss their marital ideas with him should be warm and reassuring, and throughout his discussion he should manifest a positive belief in marriage. With this emotional support from the leader, the couple may be encouraged to look into the realities that are involved in their decision to marry each other.

After they have accepted his invitation to discuss their marriage, what specific areas of marital life should the pastor concentrate upon? What needs to be communicated in these areas? I would suggest the following as a general guide.

1. *Help in understanding the emotions and personality adjustment in creating two lives into a unity.* The pastor may approach this subject first on the structural level—on the qualities of male and female and in their complement of each other. The functions of head and heart are provocative for humor and discussion, and prepare the way for insight into the nature of the marital union. The fact that insights gained in this manner may be more intellectual than emotional points up the limitations of premarital guidance. At the same time intellectual insights have their value and in the actual experiences of married life may prepare the way for the involvement of the total person.

The next level on which he may discuss this subject is that of the ways and means of communication. What do two people living together do about their negative feelings? How may they share with each other at the deeper levels of personal relating? Most of us can stand a little help in talking out our iritations on the one hand, and showing understanding toward the irritated partner on the other. The discussion may climax with a description of the spirit of forgiveness and acceptance as the bulwark that sustains the marriage during its crises.

2. *In-law adjustment.* The pastor may begin the discussion at the structural level of leaving father and mother and cleaving to the mate. The problems associated with effecting this structure can be introduced again by humor in the form of the proverbial mother-in-law problem. Whether the overtures of in-laws are interpreted as interference by husband or wife may depend on whose parents they are. There is need

to point out the danger of comparing one set of parents with the other. The value of each partner's attempting to understand the feelings of the other in these matters should be emphasized. When husband and wife are able to empathize with each other and trust each other in these parental problems, the adjustment is made with considerably less friction. It is an adjustment that should avoid the extremities of giving up all resistance to in-law interference for fear of hurting them on the one hand, and of breaking off all ties as a way of resisting them on the other. Parents have an adjustment to make also and need the understanding of their children while they are making it. The in-law relationship can and should be of great value to the couple as they draw from it the support of wisdom and concern.

3. *Relating to God.* The analogy of Christ and his Church with the marital union offers the opportunity to discuss what it means to relate to Christ. It is helpful to see how our relationship with Christ affects our relationship to ourself and to our marital partner. Since this relationship with Christ is sustained by fellowship with him, the couple may appreciate some suggestions for devotional practices, particularly practical ideas for couple devotions that are adapted to their level of religious insight. Almost everybody can read a few verses from one of the Gospels and join in the Lord's Prayer. The devotional book, *Whom God Hath Joined* by David Mace has helped many couples to begin this practice and may be an appropriate gift from the church or the pastor.[1] But devotions together should be a supplement and not a substitute for private devotions. Even though we be married, each of us retains his individuality before God, and we need to close the closet door and pray to our Father in secret. The matter of the couple's relationship to the church should also be discussed. It is as they associate themselves with the local

[1] Westminster Press.

congregations in the work and worship of God that they are members of the body of Christ and finding that meaning for their marriage that takes it over and beyond itself.

4. *Sexual adjustment and attitudes.* If the pastor can help the couple to see their sexual relationship within the scope of their life under God, he will have made his contribution in this area. The sex act grows in its meaningfulness to marriage as the marriage grows. It is conditioned not only by physical factors but by the quality of the couple's total relationship to each other. In helping them to see sex in this light he is helping them to integrate it into their married life. That which structures the sexual role of the partners is the fact that sex is a divinely designed means for the communication of married love. The woman is to receive as well as give; the man is to give as well as receive. This leads to a discussion of how each may show consideration to the other.

5. *Family plans and ideas.* Becoming married means putting oneself into the probability of becoming a parent. What thought have they given to their possibility? The pastor can help the couple to come to grips with this particular purpose of marriage—to appreciate their role as God's instruments, if not co-workers, in the creative process of being born and growing up. What is the attitude of each toward children? Do they have similar ideas? What if any are their birth control plans? If they can bring this subject out into the open with the pastor, the experience in itself may be clarifying. Where the situation warrants, the pastor may give helpful guidance from the Christian point of view regarding birth control. Here also he may want to refer the couple to a physician or clinic. As he helps them to reckon with the unpredictable nature of conception—not only in terms of preventing it, but also of achieving it—he has the opportunity to acquaint them with the avenues of help available in the community.

In applying the data of the social sciences concerning marriage and the family to the Christian understanding of the two purposes of marriage and to the parenthood role, we are able to present a basis in general principles upon which the needed personal guidance can be given. In order to secure a good beginning for the companionate purpose of marriage and its sexual expression, birth control methods may be used with profit for a short adjustment period before the onset of the complications of pregnancy. After the birth of a child they may be used again for a recuperative period in which the mother may regain her strength. During this time, controls also help to insure for the new child a reasonable period in which he can be the baby and have his infant needs for love and affection satisfied.

Each couple must reckon with their own capabilities for parenthood in their particular situation. Often this cannot be determined at the beginning but is revealed during the course of the marriage itself. The matter of health in parents and children is one consideration. The ability of parents to give of themselves to their children is another. Even as babies need most of all to be wanted, so children need most of all parents who will function as parents. The economic situation has its bearing also, but beyond the necessities of life, the economic factor is highly overrated. More than the things that money can buy, children need the things that it cannot buy.

6. *Financial guidance.* If a couple is not aware of the important role that money plays in marriage, a good time to find out is in the pastor's pre-marital guidance. What restrictions will the financial situation of the couple impose upon each? How will they accept these restrictions? How they plan to use their money will require common decisions. Are they mature enough to work together on this matter? Are they mature enough to exercise the discipline that financial limitations and marital decisions demand? Although it is the

eleventh hour, there is still time to talk about these things. Closely related to the subject is the question of whether the wife plans to work. Will her financial independence curtail her dependence on her husband and interfere with the masculine-feminine balance in the union? Will they be able to adjust to one salary when a baby comes? Are they partners enough to plan joint bank accounts? Are they able to trust each other's judgment in the use of money? When there is a week to go before pay day and all the money is spent, there is an unnecessary strain placed on the marriage bond even if one does not blame the other for the plight.

In his guidebook, *Grounds for Marriage*,[2] James R. Hines has several budgetary plans which the couple may find helpful.

Following the struggling years, money may present another problem. When the financial strains are reduced and the couple begins to climb the social ladder, this "root of all evil" may evoke a creeping materialism that destroys spiritual vitality. Nothing is so distressing to a pastor than to see this happen to some of the fine young couples he has married. While this danger may be a few years in the future, his premarital guidance offers the opportunity to discuss the Christian approach to money and the things it represents.

7. *Building the marriage.* Despite the fact that their love is genuine and wonderful it will develop throughout their entire marriage. The wedding marks the beginning of married life and like a cathedral in the making, the building will go on for a long time. Wholesome marriages do not just happen. Husband and wife have to work at it. Out of quarrels and discouragements may come insights for greater building. We do not expect to complete the cathedral the first year. Patience is needed—but a patience that gives hope rather than postponing effort.

[2] McKinley Foundation, Champaign, Illinois.

Methods of Communication

The aim in our communication of premarital guidance is to stimulate the couple to become involved in the process, to participate in the discussion, to take the initiative and responsibility for getting the understanding they need. We know that simply asking questions does not mean anybody is going to answer, and that giving answers to questions that are not asked does not mean anybody is really listening. We may need the help of some vehicle or device to stimulate the desired involvement. We shall consider some possibilities in this area.

1. *The marriage service.* There is a natural interest and curiosity over the ceremony on the part of those desiring to be married. Granted that most of this is centered in the technicalities of who says what and when, the ceremony sustains an interest that goes beyond these. The subjects pertaining to marriage that need to be discussed are contained at least implicitly in this very service. The pastor may suggest that they go through the ceremony to see what it actually says, and then at each reference to one of these subjects inquire if there is understanding here. Perhaps either the man or woman may comment in a manner that the pastor can follow up as the basis for a discussion. If not, he can give the needed understanding to these particular words of the ceremony and then continue on to the next point from which discussion may evolve.

2. *Use of questionnaires.* There are several questionnaires that have been devised for the purpose of evaluating a couple's readiness for marriage, which by this very fact emphasize the significant areas of married life. Their purpose in the pastor's premarital guidance is primarily to "break the ice." In going through the questions the couple grows curious concerning the purpose of the questions and may even desire to know more about the subject. Checking the results often provokes discussion—particularly if the man

and woman answer the same question differently. Once this has happened each wants to know how the other has answered in the remainder of the questions. If the pastor wants to use a questionnaire to begin his premarital guidance, he can usually suggest it in such a way that the couple will be at least willing and maybe even desirous to go through it. In a good natured manner he can say, "Let's see how many different ideas you have on this subject of marriage."

There are several such tests or questionnaires available for use by the average pastor who is not qualified to use the more highly specialized personality tests. Granger Westberg's *Premarital Counseling Guide* [3] is convenient because of its general scope and brevity. In his book, *Education for Marriage,* James Petersen provides one for engaged couples that the pastor may adapt with some alterations for his premarital guidance. [4] One of the most interesting for the couple is the *Marriage Counseling Kit* compiled by Hines. [5] It is composed of cards which on one side have a question about marriage and on the other side, the answer. As each person distributes the cards to yes and no piles, there is the atmosphere of a game which makes a ready springboard for discussion. Also in Hines' *Grounds for Marriage,* there is a questionnaire devoted exclusively to the spiritual side of marriage. If a questionnaire that focuses on the sexual side of marriage is desired, the *Sex Knowledge Inventory* of Gelolo McHugh is available from the Family Life Publications. [6] The test is long and the vocabulary is technical. When desired it should be used along with another questionnaire so that the premarital guidance does not become overbalanced in the direction of sex. In evaluating the results of any questionnaire the pastor will notice that the attitudes toward marriage, people, life, religion and even oneself, that are communicated in

[3] Augustana Press, Rock Island, Illinois.
[4] Scribners, 1956.
[5] McKinley Foundation, Champaign, Illinois.
[6] Duke University, Durham, N. C.

the total picture are more important than the verbal answers that may be given in any specific question.

3. *Use of literature.* The pastor may take advantage of the fact that there are many fine books written on marriage in our day and use some of these as a basis for discussion. After their inquiry about his availability for performing the ceremony, he can suggest to the couple that they take a book with them and make a date when they can return and discuss it. It is important that the pastor know the book well himself so that he can open up its main points for discussion. He may suggest that they bring written questions with them that the book has stimulated. Wood's *Harmony in Marriage* [7] and *Make Yours a Happy Marriage* by Geiseman [8] serve well in this respect. So also *The Secret of a Happy Marriage* by Burkhart [9] and *Making Your Marriage Succeed* by Adams.[10] *Sex Without Fear* [11] is excellent for its subject matter. *Grounds for Marriage* is good for the couple to read together—and answer the questionnaires. *Before You Marry* by Sylvanus Duvall [12] is advisable when the pastor has some misgivings over the marriage. The shortcoming of the literature method is that the pastor is not always dealing with people who are interested in reading or who have the capacity for comprehending what they read.

4. *Pre-Cana Conferences.* The Pre-Cana Conferences of the Roman Catholic Church deserve Protestant attention. The first conference is conducted by the priest and deals with the sacredness of marriage—the mutual sharing of life under God. The second conference concentrates on the physical side of marriage. A physician talks separately with the men and the women. The final session is conducted by a

[7] Co-author, R. L. Dickenson, Round Table Press.
[8] Concordia Press.
[9] Harper.
[10] Harper.
[11] Lewin and Gilmore, Medical Research Press.
[12] Association Press.

married couple on the day to day problems of married life as they see them. In each of these sessions there is the common format of lecture, recess and submission of written questions and discussion. Participation in these three sessions can be accepted in lieu of any specific premarital guidance.

The follow-up of the Pre-Cana Conferences is also worthy of our attention. First there are the Cana Conferences for married couples held individually throughout a year in which an entire Sunday afternoon is devoted to one of three subjects—the husband and wife relationship, parenthood with small children, and parenthood with teen-agers. Secondly, there is the Christian Family Movement in which six to seven couples meet for an indefinite number of times in each other's homes to discuss informally the issues of married life. While the priest is usually in attendance, he remains in the background until the close of the session when he attempts to clarify and summarize what has been discussed. Opportunities for postmarital guidance such as the Cana Conferences and the Christian Family Movement may be of inestimable value in relating the insights of premarital guidance to married life as it is being lived. What one *has* heard he may *really* hear when he is in the midst of a situation in which he *needs* to hear.

The format of these conferences is adaptable to a Protestant setting. So far as premarital guidance is concerned, this format has the advantage of timesaving and group interaction. On the other hand it may lack the personal application and relating of conferences alone with the pastor. Also the conference on sex might well include a minister to illustrate the integration of sex to its spiritual dimension. Larger congregations could conduct such a program within their own group, while smaller congregations could join together in a community enterprise.

Each of these methods has its own advantages in stimulating the involvement of the couple in the pastor's premarital guidance. If the pastor has a natural ability in getting openness and participation from people, he may not need any of these helps. For most of us, however, one or the other may be just the assist we need. This discussion of premarital guidance emphasizes the need for an early announcement of wedding plans. As people become accustomed to the pastor's way of doing things, they will begin to adjust themselves to his program. The advance notice he desires will depend upon how many sessions he plans to have in general with each couple. Here he may have to choose between the ideal and the feasible. I would suggest two as a minimum in which the first may include such items as practical details for the ceremony, the answering of questionnaires, or the reception of literature. He may also make it a practice to have a brief time alone with each party during this first session. In the second session he may use the results of the questionnaire or the reading or whatever other method he may choose, to stimulate the discussion on the various areas of marriage. The possibility of a third session remains if the situation warrants. When we consider the time the pastor can spend in marital counseling, time spent in some of these acts of prevention may prove to be timesaving.

Special Problems

There are times when the pastor may seriously question whether the couple should marry. Wide discrepancies in age, education, background, culture, or religion between the the parties may make the prospects for the future dim. Is he not obligated to bring his misgivings to their attention so that at least they may face with him some of the problems involved? Suppose the minister suspects that the bride is pregnant? The couple's sense of hurry—of being ill at ease in what appears to be a more guilty than normal anxiety—these and more may communicate to him the suspicion. Of course, he may be wrong. If he can see each alone, the truth is more likely to come out, particularly if he is a good listener who responds to the total communication. With a proper preface such as, "I hope you will not take this amiss since I ask only for the purpose of being of help"—he may even ask the question directly if he feels it necessary. If he gets a rather awkward reply such as, "I-I don't think so," he knows he has a pastoral problem on his hands. The reason for his inquiry is to bring the situation out into the open where its meaning for the couple can be seen. Is there a sufficient bond between the two other than the pregnancy (or the suspicion of it) to warrant the marriage? Has there been a reconciliation with God over the situation, with each other, with themselves? What weaknesses of character might have led to the moral infraction and what significance may these weaknesses have for the future? Are the parents aware of the situation—and if not, should they be?

Then there are those who have been divorced. Some ministers have a church ruling against marrying divorced people which simplifies their role. Otherwise the pastor has the more difficult task of making the decision himself. Such a decision cannot be made in any "innocent vs. guilty party" dichotomy. Marital problems are not that simple. The "innocent" party is often the one who has the pastor's ear. As a minister his main consideration is the potentiality the divorced person has of succeeding where before he met failure. The evidence of repentance—and both parties need this—with its subsequent change in attitude, is the most hopeful sign. Because of the divorced person's past experience with marriage, the premarital discussion may be most pertinent.

What about those who seemingly come out of nowhere. Usually they are in a hurry to be married. The pastor may know nothing about them except that they want him to marry them. Should he? Should he marry people when he lacks any assurance that the marriage will last? Someone about this time usually says, "Well, he might as well, because if he doesn't, they will simply go to someone else, maybe even to a justice of the peace." This is very poor logic for a minister of the Gospel. Perhaps that is where they should go—to a justice of the peace. The fact that a minister serves also as an officer of the state in his marrying capacity should in no way compromise his position as a minister of the Church. When it is performed by a minister, the wedding is a rite of the Church. No rite of the Church is performed in a vacuum; it is performed within the dynamics of the fellowship of believers. It is precisely this fact that may help the pastor to decide whether or not he should marry the doubtful couple. Is there a possibility of a follow-up with this couple in terms of the fellowship of the Church? Or are they likely to go back into that nowhere from which they suddenly appeared? A second help is the premarital guidance itself. Is the couple willing to participate in the premarital sessions? If they are not interested, this should settle the matter. If they are resistant to what the Church can offer, why should they desire a minister of the Church to marry them? When their resistance is primarily directed at a postponement of the date rather than the idea itself, the responsive pastor will help them express the reasons behind their resistance to postponement. These reasons may present the need for pastoral counseling.

When the pastor decides that he should go ahead and marry the couple, his invitation to return to him whenever the couple has need may be the most important words he speaks. This may be true not only when he has misgivings about the couple, but also when he does not. Because the invitation is backed up by the rapport established with him in the premarital sessions as an interested and understanding man of God, those who can receive least from him then may be encouraged to come to him later.

chapter IV

MARITAL CRISIS COUNSELING

The spirit that characterizes premarital guidance is one of anticipation. This anticipation makes the deposit concerning a Christian approach to marriage a focal point in premarital guidance, and the communication of the deposit the dominant motif in methodology. In marital crisis counseling the atmosphere is characterized by the emotional problem of estrangement. The deposit concerning a Christian approach to marriage has no immediate reference in this atmosphere. Rather the pastor is faced with the task of helping the individuals express and work through their problem by the methods of pastoral counseling. But the purpose behind his approach is that they may realize the divine truth regarding the marital union in their future life experiences. In other words the Christian approach to marriage is implicit in the process of marital crisis counseling even though this may not be apparent in a superficial view of the pastor's counseling procedure.

Marriage counseling has become a specialized branch of counseling. In our larger population centers the professional marriage counselor is taking his place among other members of the professional team that ministers to people in their personal needs. The pastor is not a professional marriage counselor. Some ministers may be qualified as marriage counselors, but this is not because they are ministers but because in addition to their ministerial training, they have taken the education and training for the profession known as marriage counseling. The pastor as pastor is one who among other duties does pastoral counseling with people having marriage problems. The marriage counselor is his fellow team member not his duplication. With this structure in mind let us look into the theology and theory for our practice as pastoral counselor to our people who are having marital problems.

The Ministry at the Pastoral Confessional

The setting for our task is in the pastoral confessional. The estrangement that takes place between marital partners extends its influence into the religious life: the sense of hurt and failure also threatens a breakdown in communication with God. The pastor in his confessional capacity helps a person to share that which is disturbing—to confess before God and man the rupture of a covenant with all the shock and disillusion and anxiety, guilt, shame and bitterness that accompanies it. In dealing with these highly charged emotional communications the pastor in his confessional capacity is God's own appointed minister with whom a person may unburden his soul in an atmosphere of acceptance that communicates the Gospel.

Confession implies good listening on the part of the pastoral confessor. Instead of mentally racing ahead to figure out what he is going to say as soon as the person shuts up, or going back to what has *been* said in order to figure the problem out, he must concentrate instead on what is being communicated to him in the present moment. In giving the person free rein in what he wishes to communicate by responding to his negative expressions in an understanding way and by accepting him in whatever he says, the pastor prevents any obstacle from arising in the relationship that would hinder full confession.

The pastoral confessional is a mediatorship that supports rather than supplants the priesthood of the believer. In fact the priesthood of the believer is at its very center. Through the redemptive work of Christ the way is opened into the holy of holies of God's presence. The confessional relationship is with God himself within the context of the fellowship of believers. Because God alone can make one whole, this priestly relationship with God is fundamental to the healing process. The human relationship of the pastoral confessional is a means through which the Holy Spirit operates to make Christ's reconciling work effective in the lives of people. Small wonder then that the pastor's major concern should be that he stimulate rather than interfere with the priestly potential of his counselees.

The Pastor's Goal in Marriage Counseling

What is the goal of the pastoral confessor in marital crises counseling? It is that this marriage begin to find its orientation in the great dynamic that exists between Christ and his Church. Because of this conception of marriage he sees an interrelationship between the marital and the religious life. In ministering to the marital crisis he is contributing to the religious development of the counselee and in ministering to the religious needs of the counselee he is contributing to the marital development. His task is healing and his concern is with the marriage and with the individuals. He is interested in the restoration of harmony in the marriage. But his interest extends beyond this to the growth of the individual in his own being before God—in his participation or greater participation in the new being in Christ Jesus.

Marriages grow as people do. In theological language we speak about the crucifixions preceding the resurrections— of the dips in our progress that bring on the struggle with realities that leads to the greater rises. As we hit our bottom we discover that we find ourselves. So with married life. The break in communication between husband and wife can be the dip that leads to the deep struggle and search that brings about the greater rise in intimate relating. The clash which breaks communication may lead to a deeper reconciliation that will make possible a union of greater intimacy. All of this lies within the perspective of faith in One who reconciled us to God by a crucifixion and united to himself a people by the triumph of a resurrection.

In spite of the fact that his goal is formulated by the nature of his office, the pastor is always faced with the danger of shorter goals entering in to alter his function. The most common of these in marital crisis counseling is preventing divorce. When this is our goal, we may settle for a patchwork that will hold the marriage together so far as the public is concerned. Divorce casts a bad reflection on everybody who is involved—including the pastor. It is no wonder then that he is tempted to center his task right here. After listening to a discussion on marital crisis counseling one pastor presented what he felt was a more effective and timesaving approach. "When I hear of any of my people who are contemplating divorce, I go to them and simply lay it on the line. I point out to them that if they think they have trouble now, they will find far more if they try to get divorced. Then I list all the complications that divorce brings about. When I get through with them, they are ready to call off divorce proceedings—they figure that no matter how bad things are, they wouldn't want to get into anything like that."

If divorce prevention is our goal, this pastor has a point. The heartaches and headaches that can come about before divorce settlements are completed may dwarf the original marital crisis. There is much to be said for a goal that centers in the prevention of divorce. Divorce is always a tragedy in itself. However, it may sometimes be an inevitable one, often because the marriage in the first place is tragic. Yet it is with understandable cause that Jesus accredited Moses' permission for divorce to the hardness of men's hearts—that from the beginning it was not so. A covenant made with each other and before God in which there is a pledge "for better or for worse" cannot be dissolved unless someone has already nullified it by his own actions. Divorce is never the complete solution. The wounds that ensue are deep. According to a poll of divorced people taken by the *Saturday Evening Post*, the loneliness in divorce may be as bad or even worse than the tensions of living together. But divorce may be a necessary step to a solution. From a pastoral point of view this could be the case when all efforts short of divorce have been exhausted and when the person arrives at this decision as his own.

Old Problems in New Setting

Marital problems are often simply old problems with a new environmental setting. They are problems in relating to oneself, others, and God that often antedate the marriage and are now aggravated by the frustration of marital failure. This frustration usually shows itself in resentment toward the partner. In the rupture of the relationship one is hurt and in the sense of failure he is humiliated. He may grow to hate the partner whom he feels has caused the hurt and want most of all to hurt back. In his pastoral counseling with such a person the pastor may find progress is difficult because the immediate issues in the marital crisis are so emotionally charged that they absorb the attention of the interview. Since these immediate issues are the symptoms of the failure to relate as marital partners and not the essence of the failure itself, concentration upon them—although often unavoidable—is largely a matter of releasing the pent-up emotions. To the inexperienced pastor this phase of marital crisis counseling can be very frustrating because these immediate issues of tension seem so simple a solution to an outsider. The solution is simple only because the outsider does not share the emotional background out of which these issues are interpreted by the marital partners. He cannot understand why he finds so much resistance to what appears to him to be such slight concessions to the other person. He soon finds out that it is one thing to tell the person what to do and another thing to help him. The need is obviously to get beyond the immediate issues of tension to the more basic problems of relating.

In the meantime precautions need to be taken to keep the pastor himself from becoming part of the problem. The emotional desperation that accompanies marital crises is contagious. It generates within the pastor an anxiety to produce an answer. In evaluating his own sense of failure to help preserve the marriage of a couple with whom he was counseling, a young pastor concluded that he had become too involved in the problem and the partners had grown dependent upon him to the extent that little seemed to come from *them*. How had he allowed himself to be manipulated into such a position? "I was insecure about my own role," he said. "Because of this I was very anxious about succeeding—in fact I had a need to succeed. Consequently I stepped into responsibilities that really belonged to them. It seemed nobody was going to do the things that needed doing, and so I did them. But once I began, I couldn't seem to disentangle myself."

The anxiety over "what shall I say?" or "what do I do?" is responsible for more errors of judgment in pastoral counseling than any other one factor. As pastors we need to resist this anxiety by replacing it with the guide, "How may I show understanding?" Not only is this directive less anxiety-provoking, it also provides what the counselee really needs. It structures a relationship that stimulates the counselee's own responsibility rather than replacing it with the pastor's.

The minister needs to remain in control of the number and length of the interviews in marital crisis counseling. People make many spur-of-the-moment requests to see the pastor in these crises. After one discovers how much more relaxed he feels after talking with the pastor, he is moved to call him after each new crisis—and these can come one upon another. The pastor may discover that instead of simply dropping everything to see this person, he may use the telephone call itself—providing the line is private—to give the needed release for the moment, and when this is done the person himself may suggest that he can wait for the time at which his appointment was originally set.

Marital crisis counseling is an experience with frustrations, crises and reversals galore. In order for the pastor to maintain his equilibrium he needs to realize the Lordship of the Holy Spirit in the pastoral task. He is working for and under him. The Spirit may use us to sow or to water or to reap. Naturally we would all like to reap both for the counselee's sake and for the emotional reward that reaping brings to us. But such may not be our lot. Recognizing the Lordship of the Holy Spirit takes the ultimate responsibility off the pastor's shoulders—where in our egocentrism we are predisposed to place it. It gives us a sense of control and faith when otherwise we might be driven and tossed by anxiety and panic. The pastor especially in his marital crisis counseling walks also "by faith and not by sight." When we have our role oriented in this way to the overall guidance of the chief Shepherd, we are likely to do a better task in our own shepherding. We ourselves are more open to receive because the anxiety which otherwise erupts is an interference to receiving. We are less apt to react anxiously to every new anxious communication from the marital disputants. There will also be less egocentric guilt over whether we are living up to what is expected of us—a guilt which indicates that we are working out our own problems in, with and under the problems of another.

Manner of Procedure

Because of the unique nature of marital crisis counseling the pastor's procedure in these circumstances is a subject in itself. When both husband and wife come together to see the pastor, it is usually wise for him to see each alone first. This is an assist for one to say what he really wants to say without the hindrance of the other person. The pastor on his part listens understandingly and attempts to see and feel with the person as he would in any other pastoral counseling situation in which he is confronted with an emotional problem. Later, even on the same occasion it is helpful to bring the couple together. The pastor may restate the problem as he has understood it from each in a way that expresses the feeling level of both. Since each person has had the opportunity to express himself, the possibility of a constructive session with them together is increased. However they may still begin to snap at each other, perhaps even to the point of threats and cutting sarcasm. This presents the pastor with the opportunity to help them quarrel constructively. Normally we are moved to try to keep the clash from coming about by being an arbiter who quickly puts the most charitable construction on all that is said before the other person has a chance to retaliate. When we realize we are fighting a losing battle—that they really want to fight—we may decide to let them "go to it." It is then that we resume our role as pastoral counselors. As we are understanding and acceptive toward the couple when they feud before us, they see that we are not upset by anger, nor are we critical of their behavior when they quarrel. This helps them to accept anger both in themselves and in the partner. As the sting is taken out of anger in this manner, they may be talking like sensible and sane people before they leave. Although it may be touch and go for awhile, the final outcome of the scrap may clear the air. This may carry over into their life together beyond the pastor's study as they learn how to use a quarrel constructively by ceasing to fear anger and thereby taking it less seriously.

When one of the partners comes alone to the pastor, he has the pastor's whole ear. It is only natural to try to exploit this advantage and seek to turn the counselor into an ally. The pastor must resist this overture for the sake of both of the partners. The more experience he has, the more he knows how easily his feelings about the absent partner can change when once this person has also had an opportunity to tell how he sees things. In the words of the book of Proverbs, "He who states his case first seems right, until the other comes and examines him." (18:17.) Instead of the black and white contrast between the partners that appears at the first, he may discover he is confronted with twilight zones in which he cannot be sure who is right or wrong and that furthermore it really does not make much difference. There are times of course when all the evidence indicates that one of the partners is really trying to hold the marriage together and the other obviously is not. However, the pastor is wise not to let this judgment interfere with his openness to minister to both as a pastoral counselor.

It is a human tendency to criticize someone who is not present to defend himself. The pastor cannot afford to become careless in this regard when his counselee is pouring out the resentment against the marital partner. It is a sound counseling procedure to say nothing that he would not want the absent partner to know he said. Although the counselee has no conscious intention of telling his marital partner this particular confidential bit of information, in moments of anger when in desperate need of a club, he may use it as retaliation. "Even the minister thinks you've no cause to behave as you do!" There is enough danger of our being misquoted in our counseling in these marital strifes without leaving ourselves open to being accurately quoted. Actually it is poor counseling to spend an interview in talking about the foibles of a third party. It is the counselee who should be the subject of conversation. This may seem difficult to do when the counselee is releasing resentment against the actions of the partner, but if the pastor responds not so much to the actual facts of his statements as to the feelings about what he is relating, he will succeed to some extent in his endeavor and to this extent will help the counselee. For example, after the counselee has given a particularly vivid picture of the cruelty of the partner, the pastor could say, "In doing this he has hurt you very deeply." The effect of this response is different from one that concentrates on the description itself, such as, "Do you mean he actually told you to get out?" or "Obviously he is not a very considerate person" or even, "He told you to get out."

When one of the partners comes alone to the pastor, the question arises concerning how the pastor may see the absent partner also. Should he make the attempt to contact him? It is advisable to discuss the matter with the partner who has come. Despite the breakdown in communication between them, the counselee still has the most intimate knowledge of the mate. Is there still enough rapport between the partners to sustain the counselee's suggestion to the partner that he too see the pastor? If not, does the pastor know the individual well enough to ask him to see him? If neither of these questions can be answered in the affirmative, it may be well to let the matter ride for the time being. In the meantime he can still do something for the marriage through the partner who is coming to see him—perhaps more than he realizes. After he had been counseling with a wife about her marital problems for several weeks without the husband's knowledge, a pastor was approached by the husband.

"I understand my wife has been seeing you," he said.

The pastor's heart leaped a beat as he expected an outburst of resentment. "Yes," he said, "she has."

"I pulled it out of her last night," the man said. "I figured she had been seeing somebody. She's been too relaxed—too easy to live with. I've been thinking—if she's been getting this much out of it, maybe I should see you too."

The absent partner often feels he is already judged by the pastor simply because he did not get his ear first. Nor is it unlikely that he may be the "offender" in the situation so far as outer circumstances go. It is naturally the partner who feels his position justified who is the more willing to talk to the minister about the problem. In either case the absent party may not want to see the pastor, and for the same reason. When it is necessary for the pastor to go to the absent party—and many times when all else fails to bring about the encounter it is important to make the attempt—he should go in a spirit that will reassure the defensive. The pastor needs to show the person that he is no threat to him—that he is not sticking his nose into the person's business but wants instead to be a friend to both of the partners. He must be prepared to accept the person's initial resentment at his coming and allow him the freedom to decline the invitation to talk things over. However, he should stay with the person at least ten minutes before he makes his decision to leave. Immediate declinations should not be taken at face value, for after a few minutes of further conversation, the person may change his attitude.

It is important for the pastor to establish and maintain rapport with the aloof partner. He often is also hurt—only he is not talking about it. He will be inwardly grateful for the impartiality of an understanding pastor. In the ups and downs of marital crises the pastor will find this rapport that he has established with the aloof partner a valuable ally in keeping alive the ray of hope.

Opportunities That Present Themselves

Distinct opportunities may arise in counseling with married couples because of the peculiar nature of marital crises. One is the opportunity to provide strength through the counseling relationship to do what needs to be done. Take, for an example, a wife who spent much of her time in her physician's office or in her sick bed. When her physician suggested to her that she see her pastor, he was hoping he would help her face her marital problems. The woman's mother-in-law visited her home about four days out of each week. When she arrived, she immediately took over the house, insinuating that her son needed some good cooking for a change. The wife's reaction was to become ill and retire to her bed. This simply reinforced her mother-in-law's position that her daughter-in-law was inadequate to care for her son. When the wife approached her husband about the problem, he was defensive of his mother and insisted that he would do nothing that would hurt her. The wife knew what needed to be done before she came to the pastor, but she avoided the idea because she felt unable to carry it out. The pastor attempted to create a relationship with her that would strengthen her personality to the point where she could affirm her role as wife in the presence of her mother-in-law. It was his task to keep the issues clear as they emerged from her conversation. A person who is weak finds it easy to avoid looking at alternatives or facing consequences. In an uncoercive way the pastor keeps these alternatives out in the open where the counselee can learn slowly but surely to face them.

The pastor may also have the obligation to raise the question of other possibilities with those who are contemplating drastic action. Normally the course of counseling will bring these possibilities to light, but there may not always be time for counseling to take its course. The very haste in which these crises develop may cause the parties to overlook some possibilities as they feel constrained to take immediate action.

A man who considered himself a Christian had become involved in the marital difficulties of a couple with whom he had been friends. As the man told his pastor, neither he nor the woman involved had premeditated that they should fall in love—it just happened. As far as they were concerned he either had to abandon the woman to a life with her husband which was next to impossible—and he was in no mood to do this—or prepare to marry her after her divorce. Strangely enough the woman's husband felt more defeated than angry, and was still on friendly terms with this man. Since the affair was about to break out in unpleasant scandal and the man was still sensitive to Christian appeal, the pastor suggested to him that there was another alternative. He might sacrifice his own interests and feelings and seek instead to try to bring about a reconciliation between the partners by taking advantage of the rapport he had with both. He simply sowed the idea and did not attempt to argue the point. The man began to see the challenge to sacrificial service as a genuine alternative. Although his efforts did not meet with much tangible success, he saw later what he could not see at the time—how close he had come to doing something he really did not countenance—and he was extremely grateful.

Not every decision a counselee makes in these marital crises is one with which his pastor agrees. In fact he may be convinced the decision is wrong. What then? Can he accept decisions which he does not approve? Acceptance does not mean condoning. It means the continued extension of the arm of friendship and pastoral concern; it means that the door to his office is still open. The pastor does and should have convictions. But this does not mean that he must be coercive or rejecting because of his convictions. The stronger our convictions really are, the more we are free to accept those who deviate from them.

Time often changes things—even decisions. The pastor needs to guard against his impatience to "wrap up the case." Things may have to get worse before they can get better. The growth of the people who are involved in the dispute may have to await experiences in the future. The pastor must learn the art of living with unsolved tensions, even the unsolved tensions of the couples whom he is trying to reconcile.

Time is on our side as long as we can forestall drastic action. This is why cooling off periods in these marital crises often show good results. Therefore, we can afford to have patience. Helping people see that they are in no condition to make drastic decisions when they are emotionally upset may provide the necessary postponement that initiates the conditions that may lead to reconciliation.

As a minister of the Gospel the pastor has his specifically religious opportunities in counseling with married couples. The first of these is prayer. Because of the violently negative emotions that are generated by marital conflicts, the individuals involved may find it exceedingly difficult to pray. As the pastor helps them to communicate with God concerning their burden, they are often extremely grateful. He has a good opportunity for leading them in prayer at the close of the interview. After he has finished the prayer he may find the person overcome with emotion in a combination of gratitude and shame. The words spoken by the counselee at this time may be extremely revealing—and helpful.

A second opportunity for religious help is in the devotional life. Living in a house with marital tension is nerve-wracking to say the least. Much of the pastor's counseling ministry with these people has its chief value in giving the strength to endure. But each day brings its fresh crisis. These people need daily help to stand the tensions. This can come through the devotional use of the Bible and prayer. The pastor's help in the selection of appropriate Scriptures and his instructions for prayer may be invaluable in meeting this need. In a similar way the corporate devotional life of the church service may be especially meaningful to those troubled people so long as they do not feel shut out by the stigma and shame of their problems from the worshiping community. Again the pastor's encouragement may be the deciding factor.

A third religious opportunity is the Lord's Supper. Instituted by Christ as a reassurance and demonstration of reconciliation to God, it is also an experience of oneness with our fellow believers. "Because there is one loaf, we who are many are one body, for we all partake of the same loaf." (I Cor. 10:17.) After a reconciliation has been worked out, partaking together in the Lord's Supper—preferably in the worship service or privately as a couple—helps to seal the reconciliation within the relationship of Christ to his Church. Using the Lord's Supper in this way is in line with the pattern and power inherent in the biblical pattern for marriage, as the relationship between Christ and his Church is realized ever and again in the sacrament. When in his preaching and teaching ministry the pastor emphasizes the meaning and purpose of the sacrament, his people will see its role in reconciliation and avail themselves at the opportunity to partake together.

Special Problems in Marital Crises

Sex problems. On the surface sex problems in marriage appear as frustrations over the disproportion of sexual desire between the partners. Usually it is the man who seems to have the greater desire and the woman the lesser, although this is not infrequently reversed. The sex problem must be viewed in the light of the couple's total relationship together and also in the light of the personality pattern of each of the partners.

For example we shall take Catherine and John. John was dissatisfied with his marriage to Catherine. The fact that they had two small children was not the only reason he was not even contemplating divorce. He felt he still loved Catherine. But she was not sexually responsive to him and furthermore gave him the impression that she was not particularly disturbed about the problem. When Catherine also had an opportunity to talk to the pastor, he saw that rather than being indifferent to the problem, she was defeated by it. John had made her feel something was wrong with her. As far as she was concerned he was as unsympathetic to *her* needs as he believed she was to *his*.

What does a problem of this nature have to do with religion? Why is it any concern of a *pastoral* counselor? The sex relationship of marriage is a creation of God and understanding it in this light helps us to appreciate its meaningfulness. Also the sexual barrier creates a larger barrier to the marital union as a whole because of the emotional repercussions from the frustrations and failures connected with it. In addition, underlying this supposedly physical problem are feelings and attitudes which have a decided religious significance.

Let us look first at Catherine. She could remember with some difficulty how as a very little child she would throw her arms around her parents, desiring their love, only to be thrust aside time and again with a disgusted, "Cut it out—what's the matter with you!" Rather than continue to expose herself to these humiliating rebuffs, she disciplined herself to do without a display of emotional warmth in order to maintain her self-respect. This developed into a personality trait of holding back—of being afraid to let herself go—in any situation involving personal relationships. Behind her reserve was an almost unconscious fear of showing her tender needs because she thought this exposure would be exploited. Her overtures would be spurned and her self-respect dealt another blow. Because of her reserved attitude she developed an unattractive mental picture of herself as a person. When we add to this the fact that her home attitudes toward sex which she had internalized made it emotionally repugnant to her even though intellectually she could accept its rightful place in the marital union, we have little trouble understanding why she might find it difficult to be responsive in the intimacies of married life.

John on the other hand was able to see that he had been using the sex relationship as a reassurance of his masculinity and status. The breakup of his home threw him early on his own, and although he learned to face the world with bravado, inwardly he bore the marks of his premature exposure to adult responsibilities. His was a continuous struggle with insecurity and inferiority.

Pastoral counseling with this couple can be carried out on two fronts. There is first the sex problem in itself. Regardless of how much it may be merely symptomatic of their personality difficulties, it is occupying the center of their attention and must be dealt with directly. In addition to the help that the couple will receive from talking this problem over with the pastor, there is the profit that will come from receiving some helpful information as well as inspiration regarding married love. If it is difficult or embarrassing for the pastor to discuss this subject in detail with them, he may still be helpful by assigning some reading material in the many publications in this area. Some pastors have found the *Sex Knowledge Inventory* an aid at this point. Most helpful are those insights that create within the persons a reverence and appreciation for what God intended in the sex act.

Since the sex problem rests on the underlying attitudes of the personality dynamics of each, the pastor needs to concentrate also in this larger area. For Catherine this involves relating to others, including herself, in a more open and demonstrable way. She needs to grow in her ability to let herself out and to let herself go in all of her life activities. She will be able to do this to the extent that she overcomes her fear of the possible negative consequences of such a departure from her usual defensive ways. For John it means a growth in self-respect and confidence so that he does not need to exploit the marital union for his own reassurance. Following the principles of pastoral counseling with each, the pastor can help them to grow in this emotional maturity. His own relationship to them will do much in itself. As they receive help in either area of their problem they will be helped in the other. As they grow in maturity they will grow in the deepening of their love for each other which will help to place the sex act in its wider perspective as an expression of this love and not the essence and test of it. At the same time the specific help they receive in their sexual adjustment will encourage them in their confidence and self-respect.

Infidelity. There are those sophisticated people in our society who look upon having an affair as part of the emancipated life. It is not these who usually come to the pastor's attention. If they do it is only because they have a spouse who feels differently. It is those who do not normally accept infidelity—who have some latent conscience problem over it —who may be helped by the pastor. There are two sides to most stories, including those involving infidelity. The open sin may be complicated by the hidden sin. The woman who makes life unbearable by her crotchety, faultfinding attitude or the man who leaves his wife starved for both attention and appreciation may help account for the infidelity of their partners, even if such circumstances do not excuse it. Some have lower thresholds of endurance than others. Therefore it is obvious that the pastor needs to minister to both partners even when it is only *one* who is under suspicion of infidelity.

Although there may be aggravations with the marital relationships that make one discontented, infidelity is an immature way of reacting to these aggravations. It is a flight into irresponsibility and a childish way of dealing with one's whims and impulses. Most of the time infidelity is not premeditated—it just happens. We rationalize our motivations in order to be able to follow our desires. Such self-deception goes on until "suddenly" there is the mutual realization—

"we are in love!" It can happen to anyone—even to a minister. And often it is those who could least comprehend that it could happen to them who find that it did. The judgment that heretofore they heaped on others for doing the same thing now comes back to them in mocking irony. Realizing his own vulnerability not only helps one to take precautions but also helps him to be understanding toward others when it happens to them.

The unfaithful partner is readily condemned by society, by the Church, and by the minister—and he knows it. In his own mind this puts him outside the opportunities for help that are normally open to people with problems. As a result the illicit lovers are drawn to each other for mutual support in their ostracization. In their mutual defensiveness, love justifies all. So it is two people against the snobs of society and the pharisees of the Church. In their own eyes even God may seem favorable to them. Yet they are hesitant to identify God with more than this sentimental image of one who puts his blessing on this spiritualized *eros*. Least of all are they willing to identify him with the people and teachings of the Church or even with the Bible. Law for them is rationalized away by whim, and God as love and understanding is exploited to mean God as the deified projection of their own desires.

These are the natural barriers raised to the minister in this problem of infidelity. His challenge is to get beyond these barriers, for only in this way will he be able to help these people. He does this by withholding judgment—something that is entirely unexpected by the offending parties. He shows an honest desire to understand how *they* see things. Besides being Christian this approach is good strategy from the point of view of pastoral care. It takes away the external pressure against which the offending person has been defending himself. When there is nothing to resist from the outside, the conflict goes within. When it ceases to be interfered with by reinforcement from the outside, the conscience may begin to function. In such an atmosphere, appeals to unselfish decisions are often successful. When the pressure is off and the conscience can speak, the challenge to sacrifice one's immediate desires to the values of the future and the will of God may be the deciding factor in making the necessary decision. Of course there is work to be done with the marital relationship after this decision, but the decision is fundamental to any progress.

There is always the danger that the decision to go back to one's spouse and family may be so "unselfish" in the eyes of the decider that he develops a martyr complex. However, the passage of time usually takes care of this problem. This is particularly true as the faithful spouse is helped to meet the needs of the erring one. For the immature, the period of infatuation is a very irrational time. Later when the situation changes and reason returns, the erring partner may realize how close he came to making a very tragic mistake and be very grateful to those who bore patiently with him during this irrational period. While it is true that we should do the right thing because we want to out of love rather than bowing to it in the spirit of sacrifice, we may have to accept the latter when there is no choice, in the hope that the former will develop in the passing of time.

Drinking. Many marital problems are blamed on the drinking habits of one of the partners. The question to ask is whether the drinking is a periodic reaction to the marital woes or whether it has reached the dimensions of alcoholism. Alcoholics Anonymous has its list of characteristics by which the condition of alcoholism can be determined.[1] For our purposes we can say that a person is an alcoholic when his craving for alcohol is relatively constant. He may even begin his drinking in the morning and prefer to drink alone. He

[1] The Johns Hopkins Hospital Questionnaire.

is rarely completely sober. If the need for alcohol is a thing in itself, this problem must be dealt with before the marital or any other problem. The alcoholic's state of mind is incapable of sincerity. His need for alcohol is comparable to a drug addict's need for narcotics, and he will sell his soul for it.

The pastor is wise to work with the local Alcoholics Anonymous group to help this person. He may also hope and even work for a crisis in the alcoholic's life. The possibility of the Alcoholics Anonymous being of help to the alcoholic depends on his "hitting bottom." Too often he is protected from facing the consequences of his drinking, usually by his mother and often by his wife. Of course the pastor or an Alcoholics Anonymous member may precipitate the crisis by approaching the alcoholic concerning his need for help. The opportunity may come after he has been on an extreme drunk and is aware that he has been exposed. The members of the Alcoholics Anonymous know how to talk with fellow alcoholics. If they are successful in involving the alcoholic in their weekly meetings his chances for sobriety are good. In the meantime it is helpful to the alcoholic to know that in spite of his condition he is accepted by the pastor and the congregation. He receives understanding and acceptance by the local AA—he should receive no less from the local congregation. In AA he also receives a sense of identity and importance and the opportunity to express himself. He finds meaning for his life in reaching out to others with the gospel of sobriety. When the pastor and the congregation can approximate a similar contribution to this person, the AA, far from replacing his church, will stimulate his involvement in his church.

When the alcoholic is sober he and the pastor can concentrate on the marital problem—if it has not been largely eliminated by the overcoming of the alcoholism. It is possible that marital difficulties may have been a source of tension from which he was running until his method of escape itself became the problem. As he confronts these difficulties with his pastor, the sober alcoholic may come to grips intelligently with the problem which heretofore only moved him to run. So while there may be mutuality between the drinking problem and the marital problem, the drinking problem must receive our first attention.

When the drinking problem is not one of alcoholism but rather of the periodic drowning of one's sorrows, the pastor can counsel with the person concerning these sorrows during his sober periods. In this way he is helping the drinker to see that he can develop the courage to confront his problems directly, realizing that his drinking is an escape and a sign of his emotional immaturity. These persons use drink as a crutch or a stimulant for their courage, either in meeting the demands of social relating or in propping up their sagging self-affirmation. As they grow in their development as persons before God, their ability to believe in themselves will come from their faith in God rather than from the alcoholic stimulant. If the pastor can counsel also with the other partner in the marriage, his possibility of helping them work out a solution to these difficulties is much improved. However, any growth in maturity on the part of one member of the partnership will have its good effects on the marital relationship.

The mismated. There are times when it seems obvious that the couple should never have married in the first place. Their backgrounds may be extremely diverse, their interests anything but common, and their qualities as persons pathetically dissimilar. Were they involved with the minister in premarital guidance he could do more about pointing out their potential mismating. But they *are* married and the fact that it appears that they should not have married is the proverbial "water over the dam." Yet the question may persist—should they perpetuate a mistake? What purpose is being served in their continuing to torture each other for the rest of their lives? It is good for the pastor to identify with the existential anguish of the situation so that he can face all of these questions honestly. But in spite of this identification we need also to ask—is our judgment final? Can we be sure about the future simply because we are sure about the present? If we so close the door on any possible change in the future are we not in fact limiting God? It is doubtful whether the judgment that this marriage should be dissolved is our judgment to make, even under such obvious circumstances. The pastor stands always ready to work for reconciliation.

Marriage is not something people can slough off as a broken friendship. It is not like a couple of college roommates deciding not to room together next year. Besides their legal obligations to the state there are the marital vows and the unique sharing of selves in the marital relationship. Stoic resignation to a bad marriage is not the answer. The pastor is interested in more than mere endurance of hardship. Even unselfish heroism in putting up with the mismatch is not enough. In the Church we work for something better. Granted that two people are as different as day and night, they are still human beings. And human beings have much in common. Something drew them together in the first place. Granted we often dismiss this as "merely sex," but rarely was sex the only attraction. In the beginning the individuals were, in ways that involved the whole person of each, meeting needs in the other. Even though the time for these needs may appear to be past, it may serve as a starting point if we take a second look at them. The challenge to make something positive out of the marriage will take compromise and effort on the part of both. It may even take temporary separation of bed and board. But when the pastor is ministering to Christians—with the love of the Lord in common—he ought to be able to make real progress. Even when the couple are not both Christians there is always the possibility that the time may come when they shall be. Each day brings a fresh chapter to be filled in by unpredictable as well as predictable influences.

In this whole area of pastoral counseling in marital crisis we do not want to minimize the potential in the resources of the Church. Besides the help that comes through the ministry of the word and sacrament and the corporate activities of prayer and worship, there is the experience of the fellowship of believers. Here the couple can relate to other couples who have attained a more happy marriage, perhaps through enduring these very same problems. Although the contrast may be discouraging at first, the social support of this good influence can develop into friendships beneficial for just such times as these. The common problem of involutional disturbances in marriage crises will be discussed in the chapter concerning the ministry to those in middle life. We turn now to the subject of the parent-child relationship.

chapter V

A THEOLOGICAL APPROACH
TO THE
PARENT-CHILD RELATIONSHIP

Being a parent is a tremendous responsibility. Some of us are humbled beforehand simply by contemplating the responsibility. The rest of us are humbled in the process of *being* a parent. It is sheer audacity to take the obligations of parenthood nonchalantly. Facing these obligations makes one face also his motives for wanting children. These can be as shallow or even selfish as one's motives for not wanting them.

From the Christian point of view the responsibility of parenthood involves a divine calling. This is demonstrated by the sacrament of Baptism in those churches observing infant Baptism and by the child dedication services in those who do not baptize infants. The infant is not received into the Church as an individual, even by baptism. Rather it is the parents—or godparents when parents are no longer able to fulfill the responsibility—who bring the child and promise to assume the responsibility for "bringing the child up in the nurture and admonition of the Lord." This family structure illustrated by infant baptism is part of the doctrine of the Church. The Church depends upon the family as one of its units, and it is not without some justification that the family has often been called a little church. This dependence upon the family is based on our cultural pattern in which the family is also a unit in our society. Yet the biblical emphasis upon the family and family relationships would indicate that the Church's relationship to the family is more than a mere cultural phenomenon. From the biblical point of view the family is part and parcel with the Creator's design for human living. The role of the parent in the development of a child, not merely by conception but by the parental relationship to the child, together with the difficulty in establishing parental substitutes for this relationship, have been emphasized in our day by the personality and social sciences. These provide us with further enlightenment concerning the ancient position of the Church and its Scriptures regarding the function of the family in human living.

Biblical Structure of the Parent-Child Relationship

Since parenthood is a divine calling and its obligations are also obligations to God, it is expected that the Church and its Scriptures would have something to say about the parent-child relationship. Our first thought concerning a biblical structure of the relationship would be the commandment, "Thou shalt honor thy father and thy mother." As we shall see in our study of youth, that this commandment can be abused by parents and misunderstood by children. Nevertheless the point of the commandment is obvious. Parenthood is an institution of God and children are under divine obligation to respect the position of their parents as those placed over them by God. The Bible also has much to say about the parental responsibilities to the child. When the commandment to children is quoted in the section dealing with human relationships in the letters to the Ephesians and Colossians, it is followed by a commandment to parents (although addressed only to fathers because of the position of the father in the homes of that day) which sums up the biblical emphasis concerning parents' responsibility to their children—a responsibility which is also to God. "Fathers, do not provoke your children to anger, but bring them up in the discipline and instruction of the Lord." Phillips has paraphrased the first part of this directive in the thought concepts of our day. "Fathers, don't overcorrect your children or make it difficult for them to obey the commandment, or they will grow up feeling inferior and frustrated." We have in this structure of the parental role the recognition that the relationship that ought to obtain between parent and child may be destroyed as readily by parental harshness as by filial disobedience.

Although the direction to parents probably has its immediate application in the traditional harshness of the father in the Roman world, it is structured on children's basic needs. These needs are: (1) The need for order and authority. By authority we do not mean that abuse of authority described as authoritarianism which creates conflicts over "authority figures." Rather we mean the need of children for *parents* —those who know what life in this world is about and can assert this knowledge in a leadership way. (2) Affection—and much of it. Children need tangible, down-to-earth, sincere loving. (3) The sense of belonging. Children need to know they are wanted and are a part of the family unit. (4) Capability of achievement. Children need to grow in their respective age levels into maturity and self-reliance. (5) Acceptance and understanding. Because the need for identity with the family is so strong in children, they are nourished in spirit by evidences of reconciliation and empathy in the parental attitude toward them. (6) A sense of purpose. The need of all of us to know that we shall have the opportunity to contribute ourselves to something of lasting worth is met most fully in the religious quest for the kingdom of God.

The relationship between parents and their children that is described and structured by these two commandments is initiated into existence by the parents. In this chapter we shall approach this relationship from the viewpoint of the parents' responsibility and in a later chapter discuss it from the perspective of youth's responsibility. As the relationship is structured in the Scriptures it incorporates the essential meaning of the word, discipline. Too often we think of discipline in its negative aspects of restraints and punishments.

Actually the word has its root meaning in the positive sense of leading and guiding. It is of the same word base from which we derive our word, disciple. It is cushioned by the word nurture, meaning to feed, to nurse, to nourish. Discipline, therefore, is education in its total sense, based upon the total needs of the child.

Pattern Based on Divine Parenthood

The parent who stimulates this type of disciplinary relationship with his child is following a pattern for human parenthood that corresponds to the divine parenthood. As Christians we have been given the idea of God as Father not only because he is like a human father—and we can therefore picture his relationship to us more clearly—but also because a human father has in God an example of fatherhood to emulate. This follows the familiar Old Testament pattern of relating divine truths to family relationships both as analogies for edification and as standards by which these relationships can be evaluated—a pattern that is readily adaptable to the illustration needs of preaching and teaching.

The most familiar example of this practice is the parable of the prodigal son. This is an odd story, one which most of us would have given a different ending. The prodigal made himself most unacceptable. Every person who feels unacceptable can identify himself with the prodigal—those who consider themselves to be the black sheep of the family as well as those who are considered the black sheep by the family. The father in the story is disappointed in his son's request for his share of the inheritance before his father's death, but he respected his individuality and acceded to his wishes. By that same token he took no precautions to prevent the son from reaping what he sowed. He might have become an alcoholic if he had been protected from facing the consequences of his actions. In fact many members of Alcoholics Anonymous look upon the prodigal son as a "patron saint" because it is written that he "wasted his substance in riotous living," which among other things probably included over-indulgence in the fruit of the vine. But life is an exacting teacher and the conscience is quick to pick up its lessons. After taking the bumps the prodigal finally "came to himself," which is the scriptural way of saying that he hit bottom. And bottom it was! He was forced to take a job feeding the despised swine and was not even allowed to ease his hunger pangs by eating the swine's husks.

When the prodigal came to himself he returned to his father's house. His father reacted spontaneously when he returned because he loved him unconditionally. He had thought he was dead and now he was alive. How could he help but be happy? This was good news. Not so the elder brother. His love was conditional. It was natural love—love that is given on the basis of conditions, and the prodigal brother had failed to meet these conditions. Rationally and legally the elder brother was justified in his resentment toward his father. Had *he* ever been the recipient of a celebration for being obedient? He could not share his father's spontaneous joy at his brother's return for the simple reason that he did not love him in the way his father did. Instead he wanted retaliation, and he could not understand why his father did not at least accept the prodigal's offer to do penance. Because of his attitude he could not see, as his father could, that the prodigal had *been* punished, and his return in itself was a symbol of repentance. It was to this overture for forgiveness that the father spontaneously responded.

Unconditional love is the only real love. Conditional love is a counterfeit. It says in effect, "I will love you if—or I love you because." What it means is, "I will love you if you will fulfill my demands," or, "I love you because of what you mean to me or can do for me." Natural love is based on an attraction toward those who please us; therefore it is easily extinguished. In family relationships it can lead to hypocritical offers of love. "If you would only be different, then I could love you." It is similar to hypocritical offers of freedom. "Of course the decision is yours to make, so do what you desire. But—but if you care at all for me you will do what you know I would like you to do." Such an offer fools us and yet it does not fool us; it makes us resent the person for the apparent duplicity and at the same time makes us feel guilty for doubting and resenting him. Conditional love is unaccepting. It can be shown by a hypercritical attitude on the one hand or by an overprotective, excusing, sparing attitude on the other. While it may be more obvious that an overly critical (Phillips' *overcorrective*) attitude is unaccepting, the solicitous attitude shows by its compulsion to defend that it has little confidence in the person himself.

Unconditional love is the basis for family security. When an individual is accepted as he is, he is helped to grow and to feel he really belongs to the family unit. Unconditional love is also the basis for our security with our heavenly Father. This is the essence of the Christian good news. We are not loved by God because we are lovable; rather we become lovable because we are loved.[1] Children may be blocked in receiving this love of God by human relationships in their lives which negate it. The character of the parental relationship is readily projected onto God. In the words of Fritz Kunkel:

The child cannot yet distinguish between the parents and God. To him the parents are God. The love for man and the love for God are identical. Subjectively the child does not realize that there is a choice. He accepts his parents as they are and applies what he learns from them to life and mankind and God. They are his encyclopedic knowledge of religion. Here is the point where religious education begins. If we destroy the early group feeling of our children, we destroy the basis of their

[1] Cf. Paul Ramsey's discussion of Reformational ethics in Basic Christian Ethics, N. Y. Scribners, 1957, p. 129 ff.

religious faith. If we are bad parents, the child learns that God is bad.[2]

One of the reasons why God came to us in human flesh was because of our propensity to learn through human relationships. We learn to know him through the human Jesus. But even here we block him. A group of Sunday-school children were asked who or what Jesus is like. "Oh, he's nice," they said. "He loves us—he's our friend." The second question was who or what is God like? The smiles left their faces. "Oh, he's big and powerful. He watches us all the time, and if we are naughty he punishes us." We have succeeded in drawing our children to Jesus but have alienated them from God. This destroys the meaning of the incarnation and the purpose of Christmas. We pervert Christ's Gospel as much as we pervert his person. The principal of a church kindergarten in one of our southern cities lamented the fact that she was in her most trying week of the term. "This is the week we tell the children that God loves them even when they are naughty," she said. "Parents keep calling me to object that I am undermining the discipline of the home." Conditional love seems bound to have its way!

The responsibility of not only being a parent but of establishing a parental relationship that mediates the relationship with the Heavenly Parent can lead the conscientious parent to despair. Parental guilt can be most severe, particularly in our age. With so much being written and spoken about the failures of parents, we not only have an age of guilt-ridden parents but of frightened parents. To the anxious parent it seems that one misstep may cause damage that will take eons to correct. We want our children to be "normal" so that we can feel we are good parents. But the demands seem too much. The anxious parent develops the heavy touch. He betrays his unacceptance of his children by his anxiety over

[2] *In Search of Maturity*, p. 84. By permission of Charles Scribner's Sons.

them. His is the need to manipulate them to get the desired results that would reduce his anxiety. In this manner the problems of children and the problems of parents get all mixed up together. As one parent has put it, "All the books tell us that what our children need is our love. But just when they must need my love I find them most unlovable." [3]

This parental frustration reveals the need for the parent to leave room in his thinking for the Heavenly Parent. Trust in God helps us to achieve the lighter touch with our children. The saints of God are known for not taking themselves too seriously. Child psychology is a help to the parent in preparing him for the stages in a child's development that otherwise might bewilder and disturb him. But it is faith in God that helps him to see beyond his involvement in the family crisis to the "one thing needful." With our children also we need to learn to walk by faith and not by sight. [4] Otherwise the very anxiety, guilt, and frustration that come from walking by sight become a means for the child to control the parent even if in a negative way.

Internalization of Parental Attitudes

The child learns from the attitude of his parents. He internalizes their approach to life. For this cause the parents' own growth as parents is necessary for the children's growth. Says Elton Trueblood:

The parent makes the mistake, frequently, of concentrating on the child, when he would help the child more if he would concentrate on himself. The parent must guard, accordingly, against the danger of too much self-sacrifice. If the sacrifice is obvious it defeats its purpose. Much as we help those whom we love by performing services for them, we help them more by being composed and happy persons. More good is done in per-

[3] Cf. Revel Howe. *Man's Need and God's Action* (Greenwich: Seabury Press, 1954), p. 87.
[4] Cf. II Cor. 5:7.

sonal relations by the habit of happiness than by obvious deeds of kindness.[5]

To this the biblical proverb would agree: "A cheerful heart is a good medicine"—a particularly good medicine for ailing family relationships. The Christian educator of the last century, Horace Bushnell, describes this internalization process as follows:

If the child is handled fretfully, scolded, jerked or simply laid aside unaffectionately, in no warmth of motherly gentleness, it feels the sting of just that which is felt towards it; and so it is angered by anger, irritated by irritation, fretted by fretfulness; having thus impressed just that kind of impatience or ill nature which is felt towards it, and growing faithfully into the bad mold offered as by a fixed law.[6]

In the parent's frustration over his own growth he may demand too much from his children. He does that which the scriptural directive warns against—he overcorrects. If this overcorrection is pursued relentlessly it may foster either the broken-spirited conformist whose rebellion must be carried out surreptitiously or the angry rebel whose conformity has to be equally as surreptitious. In other words parents are prone to demand from their children what they cannot be themselves. When siblings engage in bickering, the parents may be quick to silence the strife. At the same time father and mother can really go at it with each other and the children know it. Or if the children begin to complain about this or that, the parents let them know in no uncertain terms that such complaining must stop. Yet these same parents may complain about the neighbors, the relatives, the in-laws, the church, the minister or even about each other, and the chil-

[5] Elton and Pauline Trueblood, *Recovery of Family Life* (New York, Harpers, 1953), pp. 93-94.

[6] Harold Kemp, *Physicians of the Soul* (New York: Macmillan Co., 1957), p. 158.

dren have to listen. What we cannot tolerate in our children we have a way of justifying in ourselves. The father who cannot tolerate temper displays in his children cannot see the irony of it all when he himself "blows his top." "Why shouldn't I be angry!" he roars. A harried mother approached a child guidance counselor with the question, "How long does it take to get our children to follow the principles of the Sermon on the Mount such as turning the other cheek?" Said the counselor, "Madam, how long has it taken *you* to live by these principles?" We want our children to be perfect —perhaps in proportion to our frustration over our own imperfection.

Patience is different from indulgence. Patience comes from strength and decision; indulgence from weakness and indecision. A good share of our parental indulgence stems from the fear of doing the wrong thing that is so common today. Helen Eustis in an article entitled, "Goodbye to Oedipus," tells how she carefully "followed the book" in bringing up her little boy.[7] But the more she restrained herself lest she inhibit his development the more of a little monster he became. One day as they were approaching a mud puddle on the sidewalk, she thought she better take precautions. "Dear," she said, "Please don't step in the mud puddle." Whereupon the little fellow proceeded deliberately to splash right in. At that moment her natural impulses reached the required intensity to overcome her bondage to "the book," and she spontaneously cracked him across the head. Not used to such treatment the boy let out a howl of outrage. But once she had begun she knew she dare not retreat. "If you step out of line again, you'll get another one," she said. It was not long after this change of policy that her little monster became a very nice little boy. There is a virtue in being honest—even about anger.

Even children know they need limits. They need the as-

[7] *Harper's Magazine*, 206:42-8, June '53.

surance that someone is in charge. Often they will see how far they can go just to assure themselves that someone *is* in charge. They need this assurance even though they need at the same time someone to rebel against. Parents are necessary to curtail the destructive actions of their children. But this does not mean that parents must prevent their children from having destructive feelings, either by giving in to their wishes to keep them happy, or by threatening and shaming them once these feelings have arisen to the surface. Actually such procedures only serve to increase these feelings and to block any real resolution of them.

The Need to Reckon With Original Sin

The application of the Christian doctrine of original sin to the parental approach to children centers in the recognition that children have their share of evil. The challenge is to get it out into the open where it can be dealt with directly. The traditional "good boy" and "bad boy" labels can be overdone. For very young children such labels have their value in teaching what is and what is not acceptable behavior. But beyond this they can do more harm than good. Basically such typing is dishonest. Who is good? The best that we can say is that he *looks* good. What is bad? Merely the child whose badness has come to the surface. Used with any degree of coercion these labels can lead only to repression, hypocrisy, and pharisaism on the one hand or self-rejection on the other.

Motives are indigenous for Children's behavior as well as adults, and motives are not controlled by external coercions. If we parents want our children to manifest the good feelings of affection and enthusiasm we have to allow the bad feelings expression also. They are at opposite poles of the same basic emotional system and if we prevent the one pole from finding expression, we hold down the other one also. This understanding must be applied with discrimination. Not all children have a problem in expressing their negative feelings. When one child says, "I hate you!" he may best be told to be quiet. Expressions for him is not a problem—rather he needs help in controlling this expression. When another child says, "I hate you!" it may be cause for the parent to say, "Hallelujah!" The child has finally felt courageous enough to say what he has been feeling, and now can test his parents' acceptance.

One of the major challenges to the pastor in his counseling ministry is to undo the coercion that has imprisoned the expression and perhaps even the awareness of bad feelings. And this coercion can begin very early in the person's life. When the child's bad feelings are coerced into the underground they have a way of coming out tangentially. If they cannot be expressed toward their primary object—probably the parent —they may come out toward siblings or neighbor children. If the coercion prevents also this expression, it may come out toward animals. And if the repression prevents even this, the bad feelings may turn inward on the self. From the point of view of therapy the latter situation is the most difficult with which to deal. Such a child may grow up feeling inadequate and worthless. His guilt over himself—his negative mental image of himself—prevents him from achieving his self-fulfillment. Instead he may consciously or unconsciously sabotage himself and his opportunities and remain a phlegmatic, colorless personality.

Perhaps it was to illustrate this point that Jesus told the story of the sons who reacted in opposite ways to their father's orders. "He said to the first, 'Son, go and work in the vineyard today.' And he answered, 'I will not'; but afterward he repented and went. And he went to the second and said the same; and he answered, 'I go sir,' but he did not go. Which of the two did the will of his father?" Quite obviously it was the former son. So it is that when we are unable to express the resistance and resentment we have toward conformity, it in some way will sabotage this conformity. At the same time if we can express our resistance and have the satisfaction that it has been understood, we may discover that we no longer have it. We go forward and follow orders.

The Need for Parents Who Understand

Children have a need for parents who understand their needs. It is the satisfaction of this need that provides the security that helps them to cope courageously with their other needs. We can list these needs concerning which the child appreciates parental understanding as follows:

1. *The acceptance of their bodily nature and functions, such as sex and the processes of elimination, as God given and good.* We have discussed this matter in a previous chapter.

2. *The need for a support as life teaches.* We cannot spare our children the difficulties of life. Because the parent knows how he suffered as a child at school or in the neighborhood, he would like to think his child will not have these ordeals. But how else do we mature and grow self-reliant but by having to face difficulties and learning to overcome them. But if during his ordeals the child has the tangible assurance of his parents' love he has the support needed to fight his battles. Being body-soul creatures we receive the assurance of the spiritual through the physical. Although the physical demonstration of love cannot substitute for the real thing, it is the necessary conveyer of the real thing. In addition the child needs the support of the parents' example of integrity and concern for others as they meet their own demands and difficulties in the outside world.

3. *The need for acceptance as they struggle with their own evil.* As we have seen it is not natural for the parent to accept his child in failures and inadequacies, particularly if these correspond with his own inadequacies. It is as the parent receives God's acceptance of himself in his failures and short-

comings through the Christian gospel that he is enabled to give this acceptance to his children. It is at this level that we can define a Christian home. It is certainly not a home where everybody behaves like an angel or even a home where only peace prevails. Rather it is a home where the spirit of forgiveness reigns between mother and dad and dad and mother, and between parents and children and children and parents and between children and children—for we all need it. It is a home where because of this spirit there is plenty of emotional relating as parents tune in on the feeling tone of their children and respond.

4. *The need for the parents' confidence as they face their challenges.* Nothing tears down a child's confidence more than the feeling that his parents think he can do nothing right. This influence of the parents' evaluation of him never completely leaves even in adulthood. What the child thinks his parents think of him is a tremendous influence on his own attitude toward himself. He needs to know that he is liked for what he really is and not for some unrealistic picture of what the parent must *think* he is. Nor is false confidence helpful. There is that attempt to inject confidence which is so patronizing that it is obviously being offered to a weakling. Nobody is strengthened by being treated as a weakling. Another kind of false confidence leads the child to escape rather than face his difficulties. It is the kind that says, "I know my little darling could do it if he really wanted to." The "little darling" has nothing to gain from trying under these circumstances, but he certainly has plenty to lose. This is the type of escapist illusion that later adapts one to the escape of alcoholism. The kind of confidence they need is to know that the parent is feeling with them in their difficulties in the positive belief that with effort and faith things can change, and change for the better. This leaves the initiative for action with the child, and the supportive response to this initiative with the parent.

chapter VI

PASTORAL CARE
IN THE
PARENT-CHILD RELATIONSHIP

Pastoral care in the parent-child relationship is part and parcel with the pastoral challenge to present every man perfect in Christ Jesus. His task is not only evangelistic—to introduce people to the Christian Faith—but pastoral—to help them to grow in this faith. This pastoral challenge is outlined in the letter to the Hebrews:

> Therefore let us leave the elementary doctrines of Christ and go on to maturity, not laying again a foundation of repentance from dead works and of faith toward God with instruction about ablutions, the laying on of hands, the resurrection of the dead and eternal judgment. And this we will do if God permits. (Heb. 6:1-3.)

Sanctification relates to family living. As somebody has said, when a person is a Christian, even his dog should be the better for it. It is in the family relationships that growth in Christian living should take place since the way in which we relate to people is indicative of the way we are relating to God. As *I John* puts it, "He who loves God should love his brother also." (I John 4:21.)

Sanctification and Family Relationships

Even as family relationships ought to be the immediate beneficiaries of spiritual growth, they can also be the most difficult obstacles to spiritual growth. Each of us has assimilated in varying degrees the patterns for his role in his family from the patterns of his previous family. Reactions and attitudes are generated spontaneously by the occurrence of familiar situations. Our reaction patterns have developed out of family situations and are most likely to show themselves in recurrence of these family situations or situations reminiscent of them. The very familiarity we experience in our homes that makes it possible for us to "let down our hair" also makes it possible to let out our worst. It is significant that the word familiar is derived from the word family.

In addition to the handicap that these assimilations from the past may present, there is the continuum of crisis and clash that characterizes family living, testing not only the Christianity of father and mother but also their supply of nervous energy. The Vatican's apostolic delegate to the United States, Archbishop Egidio Vagnozzi, recalls that his mother had said to him as a youth, "I pity the poor woman who will marry you." But, says the Archbishop, "Almighty God took care of that." [1] But what of those of similar predispositions whom the Almighty God has not taken care of? It is upon such a sound basis that Phyllis McGinley finds her ideal in sainthood not among those in the religious orders or the priesthood who were spared the irritations of family demands, but in Thomas More who was a family man.

Of all the saints who have won their charter—
Holy man, hero, hermit, martyr,
Mystic, missioner, sage, or wit—
Saint Thomas More is my favorite.
For he loved these bounties with might and main:
God and his house and his little wife, Jane,
And four fair children his heart throve on,
Margaret, Elizabeth, Cecily, and John.

That More was a good man everybody knows.

[1] AP News, May 16, 1960.

He sang good verses and he wrote good prose,
Enjoyed a good caper and liked a good meal
And made a good Master of the Privy Seal.
A friend to Erasmus, Lily's friend,
He lived a good life and he had a good end
And left good counsel for them to con,
Margaret, Elizabeth, Cecily, and John.

Some saints are alien, hard to love,
Wild as an eagle, strange as a dove,
Too near to heaven for the mind to scan.
But Thomas More was a family man,
A husband, a courtier, a doer and a hoper
(Admired of his son-in-law, Mr. Roper),
Who punned in Latin like a Cambridge don
With Margaret, Elizabeth, Cecily, and John.

It was less old Henry than Anne Boleyn
Haled him to the Tower and locked him in.
But even in the Tower he saw things brightly.
He spoke to his jailers most politely,
And while the sorrowers turned their backs
He rallied the headsman who held the ax,
Then blessed, with the blessing of Thomas More,
God and his garden and his children four.

And I fear they missed him when he was gone—
Margaret, Elizabeth, Cecily, and John.[2]

I imagine every parent would agree that he who can be a saint in the midst of family bedlam is a saint indeed.

In spite of the handicaps, the goal in family relationships, and in particular, the parent-child relationship, is the establishment of a relationship of love as we understand it in its agape meaning. Love is also the goal of the sanctification process. It is the result of receiving the gospel. God's love

[2] From *The Love Letters of Phyllis McGinley* by Phyllis McGinley. Copyright 1954 by Phyllis McGinley. Reprinted by permission of The Viking Press.

comes to us through Christ and creates a response love within us toward God. But this response love is indiscriminate. Agape is extended to all or it is extended to none. "If any one says, 'I love God,' and hates his brother, he is a liar; for he who does not love his brother whom he has seen, cannot love God whom he has not seen." (I John 4:20.) The Church is the company of the redeemed called out (*ek-klesia*) by this love of Christ. As the fellowship of those who have received Christ's love, the Church gives this love to those within and without its fellowship, and stimulates in turn the response love to the fellowship and to all mankind. So it is that the Church is the body of Christ—making tangible his love. It is also a family—a fellowship united by agape. The implications for family living in the sanctified life are spelled out for us by Paul in I Cor. 13.

Love is patient and kind; love is not jealous or boastful; it is not arrogant or rude. Love does not insist on its own way; it is not irritable or resentful; it does not rejoice at wrong but rejoices in the right. Love bears all things, believes all things, hopes all things, endures all things.

While yet in college I was somewhat critical when the bride and groom of the wedding party in which I was involved had selected I Cor. 13 as the Scripture to be read. It seemed to me that Paul's "charity" was a description of Christian love in general and not marital love. But I now realize that it has a most direct application to marital life and that marital and family living present not only what is perhaps the area most in need of I Cor. 13, but also the area in which I Cor. 13 is most difficult to fulfill. In fact, on hearing this description of agape as it would apply to family relationships, many are overcome by a sense of frustration. The contrast between what goes on between the family members and this description of what should go on may be enough to send us into despair. It spells defeat and may create more cynicism or bitterness than anything else. The repercussions in one's spiritual life are obvious—as obvious as is the fact that family relationships are organically related to our sanctification.

The Role of Defeat in Sanctification

These defeats that we experience in applying Paul's description of agape in our family relationships can be indigenous to the pattern for sanctification from a biblical point of view. The normal abhorrence of these defeats is either a result or a cause of the distortion of the biblical view of sanctification into a legalistic and semi-Pelagian pattern for sanctification. According to this legalistic view sanctification is accomplished by human effort in regard to one's behavior regardless of how much emphasis is also placed upon the grace of God. Our defeats in showing agape have only a negative connotation in this view of santification. They are contradictions to what should be an increasing and observable ability to do better. Either we must despair in the face of such repeated defeats or place the blame on others in the family.

In the biblical view sanctification is the work of God no matter how much emphasis is also placed on human effort. And here as well as elsewhere his ways are not our ways. His strength is made perfect in weakness. Instead of the progressively increasing climb up the ladder of holiness, we have instead the continuous crucifixion of the old and the resurrection of the new. Out of defeat comes victory. God sanctifies those whom He has justified by continually re-exposing them to the justification experience. He causes them to die with Christ to their own egocentricity and to rise again with Christ from this death to the life of agape—not once, but again and again. His Spirit conforms us to the likeness of Christ by conforming us to the likeness of his death and resurrection. So it is that our growth takes place in the atmosphere of humility. A consistent and upward climb would be too noticeable to our pride. But when we fail we smite again the breast to say, "God be merciful to me the sinner." How else can we go down to our house justified?

No crucifixion is pleasant. The death of the flesh, regardless of how often it occurs, never is without its agony. Family living provides the occasion for many of these crucifixion experiences. Hence it is an area of life in which the Holy Spirit is most active to conform us to Christ. For this reason family living can lead to an even higher sanctification than withdrawing from this responsibility. The very demands and defeats it brings upon us belong to those chastenings which for the present are not joyous but grievous, but which nevertheless afterwards yield the peaceable fruit of righteousness to those who are exercised thereby. (Heb. 12:11.) As the pastor interprets these family crises in this light to those who are being exercised thereby, he will be extremely helpful to them as they grasp for some assurance for confidence and faith in the midst of the apparent wastefulness of family friction. In this way he is helping to make the Church's ministry of reconciliation a direct influence in the conflicts of family living. When our faith can see in addition to failure the potential of Christ to redeem in the midst of failure, we are moved to the wholesome experience of repentance—a sorrow with hope—in contrast to despair—a sorrow without hope—or a defensive justification of ourselves which does nothing but perpetuate estrangement. The pastor's own experience in sanctification is that which helps him to communicate the Word of God effectively to those who struggle with the same frustrations.

Agape and Wisdom

It is the pastor's understanding approach in these problems of family living that helps to break the tension that many people have over them. Naturally whatever role family living has had or is having in his own crucifixion experiences is an assist to his possessing this understanding. The goal of pastoral care in the parent-child relationship is not to create guilt. This is too easy. The goal is to stand with parents in a positive confrontation of these problems—and this is not easy. Here agape has need of wisdom.

Wisdom is exalted in the Scripture almost as much as love. "Wisdom is the principal thing; therefore get wisdom: and with all thy getting get understanding." (Prov. 4:7, K.J.V.) But the Scripture does not laud wisdom as one would human cleverness. Wisdom like love is not something indigenous to human nature. It comes through the experience of God's own self-disclosure. The writers of the wisdom literature of the Bible are not distinguished to any great extent from the wisdom writers of other religions and philosophies. Their distinction is in their own awareness that their wise sayings evolve from the worshipful experience. "The fear of the Lord is the beginning of wisdom; and the knowledge of the holy is understanding." (Prov. 9:10, K.J.V.) Nor are their wise sayings to be viewed apart from this worship experience. It is within the awe and wonder with which the creature confronts his Creator in existential encounter that wisdom has its dynamic context. Apart from this setting it is as flat as the platitudes of Polonius. From the Christian point of view wisdom is inseparable from Christian experience.

In love's search for wisdom the field of child-guidance has much to offer. Here also wisdom is incorporated within the dynamic of the Christ-Christian relationship. It is this milieu that helps to prevent the wisdom from being perverted by the fear of doing the wrong thing that it so often engenders within parents. Because of the trust that is involved in this relationship between Christ and the Christian the need to use this wisdom to manipulate the child so that our own anxieties and guilt feelings can be reduced is also lessened. What is in itself a body of relatively objective and scientific knowledge about the development of human nature is by its inclusion into the worship experience of the individual parent given an ethical and religious framework. Knowledge regardless of its source finds its most positive influence when it is involved in the wisdom that comes from knowing God.

The incorporation of this wisdom from the field of child guidance into our Christian conception of parenthood helps us to interpret God's structure for this relationship to our day. Where a previous generation interpreted Christian parenthood in terms of strictness regarding external behavior —and perhaps rightly so—our generation needs to hear it interpreted in terms of affection and understanding and the increasing extension of freedom in respect for developing individuality. But affection and understanding do not imply indulgence. Children have a need for limits and for parents who exercise this guidance by knowing their own minds. This wisdom gives us a clearer interpretation of what offending one of these little ones means. It means a denial of the satisfaction of the child's basic needs on the part of those who in our society alone can give it. But knowing what these needs are in itself may not be enough. The parent may not be able to follow through on the wisdom because of the poverty within his own personality. Here is where santification is important in relating wisdom to agape. In the parent's own growth in relating to Christ and his Church— a growth precipitated by crucifixions and resurrections—he grows also in his ability to reflect God's love—to give of himself to his child.

Regularly Scheduled Ministries

Where premarital guidance and pastoral counseling in marital crises have their times appointed by the occasion of need, pastoral care in the parent-child relationship is conducted for the most part through the regularly scheduled ministries of preaching and teaching. In his sermons the pastor may carry out this ministry by making the application of sanctification to family relationships whenever his text would warrant. The family imagery which characterizes the religious teachings of the Bible—which we shall discuss shortly—offers another opportunity to give specific help. Conducting a sermon series on the Christian home is an effective way of conducting this area of pastoral care. Also special occasions such as Mother's Day present an opportune time for sermons on the parent-child relationship. Not only is this the psychological moment so far as the hearers are concerned, but it allows the preacher to recognize the day without having to indulge in mere sentimentality.

So far as teaching is concerned the ideal opportunity is in the parents' class of the church school. Here is a natural group situation for a mutual sharing of the concerns of parenthood with the deposit of knowledge about the theological approach to the parent-child relationship to serve as a background or stimulation for discussion. What is simply a series of facts when presented as a lecture can become emotional insights when discussed in a group that shares the common concern.

Another opportunity for teaching is to conduct on occasion a family clinic similar to the second session of the Cana Conferences. The outline for this Sunday afternoon program is as follows.

    I. Brief background—the husband-wife relationship (Cana I)
    II. Vocation of Parenthood
    III. Understanding the Infant and Pre-school Child
    IV. Teaching Religion in the Home
    V. Teaching Right Attitudes in the Home
    VI. Sex Instruction in the Home

VII. The Child's Psychological Needs

VIII. The Problem of Discipline.[3]

Perhaps one of the church organizations such as the Couples Club could sponsor such a conference. Perhaps it can be done in co-operation with other churches in the community.

Our immediate reaction so far as pastoral care is concerned is probably similar to the lament of a Cana priest with whom I talked—that it is those who should attend such a conference that do not. However I would submit that this is not necessarily so. The openly selfish or indifferent parent is the one less likely to attend. But he may actually be causing fewer conflicts in his parent-child relationships than the parent whose concern is one of egocentric anxiety. At least the child of an openly selfish or indifferent parent knows where he stands and has few guilt problems over his resentment toward his parent. But how can you resent the parent who is obviously so concerned about you without feeling like a cad? This anxious parent will usually be in attendance at such a conference. His anxiety in itself is a sign of need. Often these anxious people are our conscientious church members. Naturally the pastor would like to reach beyond his faithful members. But let us never forget that our faithful members may need help. The pastor often confuses church loyalty with sanctification. My work in pastoral counseling has been largely with the children of faithful church members. They need help because there are plenty of family problems among the faithful, although they are often hidden, even from the pastor. The very fact that the family is supposed to be a good family because of their faithfulness in church activities makes it all the more confusing to the children who experience the lack in wholesome and emotionally satisfying relationships within the family.

In each of these opportunities through preaching, teaching

[3] *The Cana Conference* (Proceedings of the Chicago Archdiocesan Study Week), pp. 97-100.

and group work for pastoral care in the parent-child relationship, the characteristic of the Bible to relate its message in family terms gives the pastor a ready application for divine truth. There is for example the character of God as Father which we discussed in our theological approach. In our specific application in pastoral care this Fatherly character of God is demonstrated by the very agape and wisdom that characterize our growth in sanctification. In God we see the pattern for the parental agape. God gives himself to his children—this is the essence of the gospel message. Yet he allows these children to suffer. He is able to remove their crosses, but he often does not. He knows that these sufferings are inseparable from their struggle with the ultimatum of life to grow up or perish.[4] It is precisely because his love is unconditional that it is demanding. He who first gives all also demands all from the recipient. The fact that he gives us the full assurance of his love freely is the source of the security of soul that is the basis for growth. The fact that he demands that we cope with the full brunt of life's challenges is the stimulus which provides the crucifixions and resurrections that develop not only a sense of responsibility and maturity of judgment but the opportunity to give of ourselves as well as receive from others.

So God's parental agape sets the stage for his parental wisdom. He is desirous to give to us. Yet he awaits our asking. Initiation is indispensable to growth. He is able to do for us—yet he depends upon our doing. It is in our own assumption of responsibility for action that our character develops. He offers us the affectionate and tangible assurance of his love in the sacrament. Yet he sends us forth from the protected atmosphere of his house into the world outside where the battle has to be fought. Of what value is the security of home if it does not equip us to meet life in the larger world without?

[4] Cf. F. Kunkel, *In Search of Maturity*, p. 192.

Personal Counseling

When individual parents are emotionally disturbed over their parental role and worried about the development of their children they may seek out the pastor's help. This is particularly true in those congregations where the pastor has been executing his pastoral care in the parent-child relationship through his preaching and teaching ministries—where he has related the necessity of meeting a child's emotional needs to the child's spiritual growth and has related the parent's spiritual growth to the parent's growing ability to meet his children's needs. When they realize that these problems of parenthood are related to their religion and that the pastor has an interest in ministering to them in this area, they will come to him when frustration overwhelms them. Prepared by this atmosphere they are likly to be very grateful to have someone discuss their children with them and to be open to receive help—even criticism.

When parents come for personal counseling in their parenthood role the pastor would follow the same principles of pastoral counseling as he would with people having emotional problems. This means that he would encourage the parents to express their anxieties, guilts and perhaps even resentments regarding their children. These very emotions that arise out of our parental frustrations complicate the problem and worsen the relationship with the child. As catharsis continues the parent may bring to light also some marital conflicts, since children suffer emotionally and become behavior problems when there are open or hidden tensions between father and mother. In fact it may be the guilt over these conflicts with the mate that causes the parent to react with such anxiety to their effect on the children.

In addition to the release and insights that may come from his counseling the pastor may offer some helpful information concerning children's needs when the parent appears open to receive it. This may come in the form of helpful literature to read such as Baruch's *New Ways of Discipline* [5] or Beecher's *Parents on the Run,*[6] depending upon the nature of the problem in the parent-child relationship. A pamphlet for teachers entitled, *Teacher Listen, the Children Speak,*[7] is excellent for parents as well, helping them to interpret their children's behavior. After the parents have had the chance to digest this information, they may find it profitable to discuss with the pastor whatever emotional resistances or blockages they may have discovered in attempting to carry out the principles of child guidance—those resistances that prevent them from giving to their children what they know the children need. Here the counseling process comes to grips with those blind spots in our way of looking at things which are usually defensive measures, and also those assimilations from past family experiences that hang over to handicap the parent in his present responsibilities to his child. As the nature of the difficulty is revealed the pastor may feel it is wise to refer the parent to a child guidance clinic if this resource is available in the community, depending upon the apparent gravity of the problem, particularly as it relates to the child.

Pastoral Visitation

Pastoral help in parenthood is initiated, undergirded and perhaps even carried out by a faithful and regular visitation by the pastor into the homes of his congregation. Here he sees his people in their family setting, and as a family they receive him into their homes. How better can he know them

[5] Dorothy Baruch. *New Ways of Discipline* (New York: Whittlesey House, 1949).

[6] Marguerite and Willard Beecher, *Parents on the Run* (New York: Julian Press, 1955).

[7] James L. Hymes, The N.Y. State Society for Mental Health, 105 E. 22nd St. New York 10, N.Y.

or they him? Perhaps something comes up during these visits regarding the family relationships. Perhaps it does not. In either case the visit has a stabilizing effect in these relationships. Pastoral visitation is an intangible way of relating the gospel to family life. More than just a friend has entered the home. The pastor represents the Church and by the very fact that he represents or symbolizes the Church to these families, he communicates in ways that cannot always be perceived or planned what this Church offers and what this Church stands for.

chapter **VII**

A THEOLOGICAL APPROACH
TO YOUTH

What's happening today with our youth? Those who ask this question are not simply old fogies who forgot what it was like when they were young. Today's youth problem is not just the old wrapped up in a new package. The juvenile delinquent today is the young criminal. Young people's pranks show a wanton disregard for basic human decencies. The traditional lack of respect for the old has been shocking in its savage and even sadistic manifestations. Some believe it is the result of World War II. We cannot expect to break all the laws of God on a global scale and not seriously corrupt our culture. Others see it as the evidence that we are living in a post-Christian age. The first generation that breaks with its traditional Christian roots is still largely influenced by its heritage. But the second and third generation of those who have broken away show a basically new nature which is characterized by this complete lack of Christian influence.

Up until recently those who wished to refute these attempted explanations could point to France and Italy. Here were two countries that had suffered more from the war than had we and had so broken with their historic Christian ties that each had communist parties which threatened to claim the majority of the voters in free elections. Yet Italy and France had almost no problem with juvenile delinquency. What they had, however, was family solidarity, and in this we Americans are lacking. But now France and Italy are being shocked by the rise of a new problem—but no new one for us—youth terrorism. The conclusion is that the family unity that has characterized these old world cultures is disintegrating. Regardless of how we may attempt to account for the present distress, the youth of today present a big challenge to the pastor.

Confronting the Existential Anxieties

Although our current youth problem is something new, it has grown out of the fact that adolescence is by nature a time of turbulence. The adolescent comes slowly but surely into the awful realization that he is a self, cut off in the depths from all other selves. He is brought by his development into the terrifying realization of what an uncertain world this is. He is confronted with road blocks and blind alleys but "no exit." In experiencing the nakedness of existence, the "nonbeing within being" looms up to threaten him. The experience is best described by Tillich's ontology of anxiety.[1] Tillich says that there are three types of anxiety that go with human existence. They are created by the three directions in which nonbeing or destruction threatens being or existence. The first of these is the anxiety over fate and death. The finality of death seems to extend its terminal qualities back into life, and the reality of nonbeing's ultimate victory over being is as apparent as it is in a corpse. The second is the anxiety caused by emptiness and meaninglessness. The meaning and purpose for living that a child assumes, an adolescent questions. When the spiritual quest for meaning finds only negative answers, the human soul is consumed with an agonizing emptiness. The third is the anxiety of guilt and condemnation. The human being discovers he has not only the freedom to act against his own destiny, but also the necessity to stand in judgment upon his use of this freedom. The result

[1] Paul Tillich, *Courage to Be* (New Haven: Yale Univ. Press, 1952), pp. 32-64.

is the negative judgment which we know as guilt. The anxiety is over the condemnation that guilt implies.

These are the anxieties which plague the human being simply because he is a human being in our kind of existence. Having had little time or experience in which to build up a defense against these anxieties, the adolescent more or less stumbles into them with his guard down. His reaction may be similar to that of his mother or father as they approach the involutional period of life, when these anxieties may erupt again in their full intensity. In each instance it is the necessity of entering into a new era of existence for which one feels inadequate, that causes the destructive forces within life to loom up with increased foreboding.

This inner turbulence erupts in all manner of religious questions. Young people know they need a faith to live by. But their expanding intellectual powers appear as a threat to any religious faith. In addition, problems that disturb them emotionally also disturb their religious life. They have a real need for religion's integrating powers to make sense out of all their disjointed discoveries and to quiet the anxiety and conflict within. Naturally they have had these existential anxieties before in their embryonic stage, but now the development of their potentialities has made possible a full-blown confrontation. Some may have had some of this experience even in childhood where for some very definite reasons they had difficulty in accepting their existence. These are the children who have not known the cohesion of being indistinguishable from the family group, because the elementary family ties that give such cohesion to most children have not existed for them.

The faith of a little child is easy when there is this cohesion with the family group. Not only can he believe in the omnipotence of God, but he even believes in the omnipotence of his parents. The world of imagination in which he lives offers a congenial habitat for faith. But it is not so in the adult world. And between the childhood faith and the adult faith there is a traumatic transition. It is unrealistic to expect child faith in an adolescent who is facing the realities of justified doubt full force.

Guilt and Sex

The guilt that is the inevitable concomitant of adolescent development warrants further investigation. The growth into individualization throws the adolescent in upon himself, as the rise of normal anxieties preoccupy his attention. Because of this he develops a defensive self-centeredness in his motivations which moves him to exploit others for his own advantage and to feel himself in hostile conflict with others when this advantage is threatened. Although he feels helpless to alter this self-centered exploitation of others, he feels guilty over it. This guilt is aggravated by the fact that physically he is neither here nor there. He feels awkward in both appearance and bearing. If he is behind others of his own age in his development, he is even more distressed over himself. To add to his discomfiture, he may have the familiar adolescent disfiguration of pimples or acne.

The advent of puberty adds a new threatening force to youth's self-esteem. He becomes sexually sensitive. The potential which he heretofore has experienced in part now comes to the fore with such intensity that it can confuse him. The close affinity of guilt for sex has been demonstrated ever since Adam and Eve in the Garden of Eden sought to relieve their guilty conscience over rebelling against God by covering their nakedness over which they now felt shame. This very guilt over sex may augment sex to the proportions of an uncontrollable power, and what one senses is beyond his control he grows to fear. Sex can become identified with the nonbeing that threatens to destroy us.

This is more likely to occur when certain environmental

factors cause sex to become a plaguing compulsion. One of these is the semi-pornographic literature which is becoming increasingly available to young people in our over-stimulated sexo-centric age. In contrast to this overstimulation which is more or less sub rosa, his own home environment may intensify his curiosity in the opposite direction. Here in the family circle the normal free atmosphere that an adolescent needs to learn about his own and the opposite sex may be stifled by a well-meaning but nevertheless prudish attitude toward the body and its functions. Should the adolescent's rebellion against his family be extreme, he may fix on sex as an outlet for his defiance of accepted mores.

When youth are malnourished in their natural need for love and affection, their sexual desire may be intensified in protest. This is because God created sex as a means for intimate relating. The increased sexual agitation is symbolic of youth's desire to break out of his emotional isolation and to unite with another. The direction in which this maturing desire is pointed is normally toward the opposite sex, although should that desire encounter serious obstacles in this normal maturation, it may also be toward the same sex. If their social experience with their own peer group is as devoid of emotionally satisfying relationships as their home life, they may turn this desire in upon themselves and use masturbation as a compulsive substitute for wholesome personal relationships. But the guilt they often experience because of their addiction to masturbation only increases their sense of isolation.

Sex is a representative of the many new things that are opening to youth, dramatizing ever anew the age-old temptation of Eve. Within the woman the serpent sowed the suspicion that there was something in life she had not yet experienced, and that she would not be really living until she had. The adolescent is disturbed by the same suspicion when he hears that, "everybody's doing it." An intense curiosity develops to find out what these expectant thrills are. Here is the attractiveness of evil—it offers a new dimension to living that at the moment seems to be everything. "In the day ye eat thereof ye shall be as gods." Small wonder that young people develop an inferiority about not having all these experiences—and fuel is added to the fire of the most acute inferiority of all, namely, the inferiority over oneself as a person. To be so unadventuresome and green implies that one has a dull or at best an uninteresting personality. We are face to face with the apparent dilemma between having to be remorseful over "the sins of our youth," and having to be regretful that we did not really *live* in our youth.

Need for Social Support

Young people have a strong need for social support. They need this support from certain strategic adults who represent to them the adult world. They need it from their own peer group which also has its more important personages. When this support is threatened, the world of the adolescent is severely shaken. The hysteria over little social dilemmas that characterize the girl or the intense interest in sporting events that occupy the boy may seem a strange contrast to the anxieties over the great issues of existence. Yet it is precisely because youth are confronted by these major anxieties that these apparently superficial interests mean so much. In being a part of the social elite or in being engrossed in the activities of athletics, young people are absorbed in what seems to them to be the insurance against the frightening specter of being a nonetity.

But not all youth react the same to their common crises. There are two extremes for which the terms introvertive and extrovertive still have descriptive value. Those who tend to meet life introvertively are more socially withdrawn, usually because the social challenge is too much for them. They are more introspective and reflective. Although their existence is more painful, they are also likely to be more aware of their problems. Because of their approach to their crises, they tend to develop more vertically than horizontally. For this reason they may have more depth to them and because of this they have greater promise. But introvertive people can avoid reflecting upon that which is painful by becoming involved in the world of things in terms of solitary pursuits.

The extrovertive youth to all appearances has an easier time in adolescence than his introvertive counterpart. He is more easily distracted from inner conflicts because he involves himself actively in interpersonal activities. Because of his horizontal development he may be less of a problem solver in the final analysis than the introvert. Too much surface involvement may mean too little reflective activity and little depth of soul.

So far as the need for social support is concerned, the majority of youth are in-and-outers. When they are in, all is well with the world, and when they are out, the world's against them, and they go into a mood or become aggressively hostile. This strong need sets the stage for a common religious problem. The mores of the peer group with which the youth wants to identify himself to enhance his prestige, may not be in accordance with the mores of the important adults in his life, or even more important, with his own conscience. In this tug of war between the two, which will give?

Rightly or wrongly young people as well as others tend to identify their conscience with the voice of God. When they violate it they interrupt their dialogue with God. Although they may do so for social advantages, the result could be a loss religiously and even socially. There is no clear-cut division between the social and religious life. Our dialogue with God helps us to establish a dialogue with others. Without it youth's social life may be more characterized by externalized corporate activity than by any social dialogue. What is gained in immediate social support may be at the expense of long-range social or personal depth.

On the other hand if young people sacrifice social support for conscience, they may experience a damage to their own self-image which their peer group helps to support. If their dialogue with God is not of sufficient stability, this socially damaged self-image may hinder their reception of God's acceptance. If their dialogue with God is of sufficient stability, the obligation is still before them to establish social ties. When the religious relationship exists without supporting human relationships, its very nature may become distorted. In isolation it may be used as a compensation for other relationships. When this happens it becomes something other than a dialogue with God—it becomes at least in part a dialogue with oneself. What shall be the place in one's life of such a compensatory distortion of the religious dialogue if and when social ties are reestablished?

Rebellion and Disillusion

Adolesence is a time of inevitable rebellion. Youth has the need to come out from under the authority he still wants to believe in. One of the most obvious things about man is that he believes he is free or should be free, and he resists unrelentingly any attempt arbitrarily to deprive him of this freedom. At the same time youth is frightened at the prospect of being an adult. He is confronted with the existential dilemma of freedom—desiring its privileges and resisting its obligations. Although he is on guard against any obvious show of desire to return to childhood, it comes out in indirect ways and at unguarded moments. He attempts to hide his insecurity with a bold front—by aping adult ways externally and by going in gangs for support.

Throughout his rebellion the adolescent is looking for an ideal to pull him through the dilemma of it all. The trouble in our day is that youth seem so often to have given up hope of finding this ideal in our adult world. They are finding it instead in their own peer group, where unfortunately the tie with the past heritage is weak. But the potentiality for establishing their ideal in the adult world is still present, and when challenged, has the danger of turning into hero worship. Sometimes the hero who is worshiped is the minister. When asked about her religious beliefs, a freshman coed said, "I believe whatever my minister tells me to believe. He's—well he's just a wonderful guy." Obviously youth's adultation of the adult hero can be very unrealistic. The result is that they can become extremely disillusioned when they discover that their idol has clay feet. The more insecure they are, the less they can stand any imperfection in their hero. In their disillusion the bottom drops out of their world and they feel they can never have confidence in any adult again.

This disillusionment with the ideal adult begins with disillusionment over parents. Such disillusion is almost inevitable because, as a child, the youth had unavoidably overrated the parent. This overrating of parents is part of the delusion of the unreal world in which a child lives. When parents fight against this disconcerting disillusionment of their adolescent toward them, they antagonize the situation. As a result of their resistance to his attempts to reduce them to size, the youth will either repress his disillusionment or he will lash back all the more rebelliously. Of the two, the latter is the more healthy response.

The trouble is that regardless of how the adolescent reacts to this parental antagonism of his rebellion, the Heavenly Parent gets mixed up in the fracas also. It is difficult for young people to draw any sharp distinction between their own parents and the Heavenly Parent, at least emotionally, and their rebellion against their parents may extend to the Heavenly Parent in all manner of wildness in behavior. It may be extended also to life as a whole in the form of daredevil exploits. These are daring attempts to penetrate the existential anxieties. Against the anxiety of death and fate, he may see how close he can come to death, attempting in a sense to gain some control over it and to overcome his fear of it. The familiar search for kicks and thrills is an attempt to mitigate the anxiety of meaninglessness and emptiness by filling the void with some sort of immediate meaning. To quiet the anxiety of guilt and condemnation he may play recklessly with his life as a symbol for the shedding of blood, as a type of radical atonement.

The crucial element is not the rebellion, but how the rebellion is carried out—whether it is expressed outwardly or forced to confine itself to inward fantasies, whether it is a creative phase in the development as a person or a destructive phase, blocking his maturity. Rebellion in youth is a manifestation of the developing self. Theologically it is the transitional stage from an "outer-directed" and "tradition-directed" faith to one that is also "inner-directed." It is the development in creation which lays the foundation for the development in redemption of the priesthood of the believer. Normally, if the rebellion is not met with too much resistance, it works itself out constructively, but where it is met with overpowering resistance, the adolescent may bog down in it. It may be helpful to note some examples of how normal rebellion becomes abnormal because of this interference.

John's father was a strong-minded overbearing individual with "the Lord on his side." Always he could show where he was right. John could either greatly admire such an imposing figure or face his glaring weaknesses and shortcomings. He chose the former, subconsciously of course. Being the oldest in the family he had to pioneer in this father-son relationship. Because of the course he had elected, John experienced no conscious revolt. Instead he desperately held down any such tendencies by emotionally defending his father at every turn.

He became a carbon copy defender of all of his father's ideas.

Bill had a very religious and overly strict mother. Hers was a pietism that was warm in faith and strong on the law. Bill rebelled extremely against the legalism in her pietism, developing a passion for the Bohemian life. On the other hand he was unwilling to let go of her warm faith. But he met the greatest resistance within himself in making the necessary decisions that would unite his faith with morality. As a result his inner life was plagued with terrible feelings of estrangement.

Sam found acceptance in being the model son. Adolescent revolt came but not outwardly. Sam was aware of his inner revolt but he feared that any expression of it would cause him to lose his halo of parental respect. So he went through the motions of conformity, but his heart was not in it. Everything he did, he did because he felt it was what his parents wanted him to do, and not because *he* wanted to do it. By indirectly sabotaging himself through lack of effort and loss of incentive, he carried out his rebellion passively, until finally he realized that if he was ever going to be a self, he would have to strike out actively on his own, even though it meant rejection by his folks. This would take courage. Sam felt that for him it meant that he must drop out of college and join the army. This was a drastic step, but perhaps it was better than to end up as one man I knew who felt he would have to wait until his father died before he could release himself to do his best. He was so bound by unexpressed revolt, kept within by a combination of awesome admiration of his father and a fear of hurting him, that he was not able to let himself go in the direction of his own fulfillment. Here is unfinished emancipation—an unrealized life.

From our realization of the needs and dynamics of youth, it is evident that youth is a time of great theological significance. Although our point of reference has been on the nature of adolescent development as seen from a pastoral point of view, rather than on specific biblical references to youth as was advisable in the discussion of the Christian approach to marriage and the parent-child relationship, the biblical position is still very much in evidence. The existential predicament of youth is simply an extreme revelation of the predicament of man and of his need for the good news of Christianity. Youth's need for reconciliation, fellowship, faith, self-affirmation, and creative dedication stand out sharply in our study. Of equal importance is the fact that the nature of youth and the character of his needs point to the ways in which the Church and its ministry as it is represented in the local congregation, can exercise its pastoral care for the wholesome development before God of the young people within the reach of its influence. It is to this task of the functional approach that we now turn.

chapter VIII

PASTORAL CARE OF YOUTH

From our pastoral perspective of youth it is very apparent that the pastor should be an important person in the lives of the youth both within and on the fringe of his congregation. He is the representative of the Church and in a sense also of God and is qualified by both education and ordination to minister to them. But he does so clearly as a minister of a congregation, and the resources of the congregation, its fellowship, its worship, and its organization are his indispensable allies. Yet it is he who is the leader, and the character of the resources will be largely determined by the quality of his leadership.

The Importance of
the Pastoral Relationship

The pastor's challenge is to establish the pastoral relationship with each of his youth. This relationship could be the vitally needed tie with the adult world and the heritage of our past for this drifting younger generation. If he is to meet this challenge he cannot afford to succumb to the fear of young people so common today. Many ministers go out of their way to avoid youth work, and with good reason. It is hard and it can be discouraging. More than with any other group within the church the pastor fears he may fail with the youth, and if he can get some assistant to take over this area, he is understandably tempted. But this very fear we have of youth becomes a power in their hands, and power corrupts. It is a power they know they should not have and because we have given it to them they only disrespect us more. We are the adults, not they. We are the ones they need to respect, and how can they respect adults who fear them? The disruptive youth in the youth group does not like himself or his minister when he is allowed to sabotage the meeting, simply because no one knows quite how to deal with him. He needs to be shown in a firm but understanding way *in private* what can and cannot be done. It is in his pastoral care of youth more than anywhere else that the pastor has to reckon with the Scripture that "there is no fear in love."

The pastor is the vitally needed tie with Jesus Christ. For all of his divinity Jesus is a man and a leader of men. In his Palestinian ministry he challenged the devotion of disciples, most of whom were young men. He is still capable of challenging the devotion of youth in a master-disciple way. But he is no longer with us in his visible presence. To make up for this shortcoming he has established his Church, which Paul significantly calls, "Christ's Body." It is through this fellowship of believers that the tangible reality of the person of Christ becomes known. As the ordained minister of this fellowship the pastor is in the forefront of this function of the Church. He leads people to Christ through himself. Because of their need for adult inspiration there is perhaps no area of his ministry in which his own person is so important for this task than in his ministry to youth. For the same reason there is no area which tempts him more to exploit this role for his own needs.

The pastor must be careful about exploiting youth in his teaching ministry. Because of their respect for his religious knowledge, they are easily fooled by half-truths. But when they find out the whole truth, they may become cynical of any religious truth. As teachers of religion to youth we are tempted to oversimplify problems of belief because we fear their latent skepticism. Because it arouses our own latent skepticism when it comes out and leaves us feeling inadequate to cope with it, we may do all we can to keep their skepticism from coming to the fore, even to the point of giving a false impression by presenting only part of the total picture.

We also know how susceptible they are to guilt over sex and parental problems. This awareness presents a real temptation to us when delivering inspirational addresses or sermons to youth. It is easy to exploit this tender sensitivity of theirs for some tangible and supposedly religious end. Now it is we who are corrupted by power—the power we know we have over them in these matters. We know too that their excessive need for social support makes them susceptible to idolatry regarding social acceptance and popularity. It is easy to hit them hard here and make them feel very guilty. But may it not be unfair and even dishonest?

The task of the pastor does not lie in the direction of exploiting youth's vulnerable areas, but of convincing them that we would be understanding no matter what they would confide to us. To do this we need to avoid the typical parental, moralistic approach, which simply tries to reinforce the shaky regime of an old and worn out legalism. It may be safest to follow the party line on what should and should not be, but it is not the way to show young people that we would *understand* their side of it, regardless of whether we would personally agree with it or not. Sensing the stuffiness of the old approach some pastors have tried to capture youth's confidence by going to the opposite extreme. In order to avoid a forbidding parental role, they divest themselves of all semblance of adulthood in order to identify themselves with the youth. They are trying to create an impression which they hope will cause youth to like them. But by following this way of identification, they lose the possibility of helping young people as much as they would had they assumed the pose of conservative rigidity. Youth need and want an understanding adult, not simply an understanding adolescent. When the pastor identifies himself with the level of his youth to the extent that he becomes one of them, he becomes merely another competitor from their peer group. While they appreciate his being flexible enough to play ball with them, they would like him to appreciate their home runs more than they appreciate his compulsion to have to hit one himself.

A Religion That Is Helpful

Young people need a religion that will help them meet their problems where they are living. If ever religion needs to be existential it is when one is so painfully conscious of one's own naked existence and isolation. Youth is a time of inward suffering and God speaks through suffering. The solidifying or hardening process of maturing age is not yet a hindrance to youth. They are open to hear and to receive. The pastor's unique opportunity is to communicate the gospel to them where they are listening. Faith, as a leap into the dark, is softened and enlightened by the understanding of a Heavenly Father's love communicated by words and by a relationship of concern. In plain language they need a God whom they can know. Their heightened need to relate to persons is true religiously also. In this way they find a solution to their guilt and a sense of calling for their future.

This need for the personhood of God must be emphasized in spite of all the warnings from those who are afraid that a God who is a person is a God who is too small. Youth may have to know the God *in-front-of* the *God-behind-God* before they can ever know how the God-behind-God can transcend him. The need for a God to whom they can relate in a personal way is youth's challenge to the pastor. The pastor's approach in meeting this need is twofold, and each is needed for the success of the other. On the one hand he can help them to establish a personal relationship with him as a man of God. In this way they are helped to know the God behind the man of God. On the other hand he can attempt to apply the Christian message to their problem areas. These areas can be roughly centered around the following six.

1. *Social problems.* Youth need all the help that their faith in God can give them in the ups and downs of the satisfaction of their need to be a part of their peer group. But this phase of the problem is no more disturbing than the conflict created by the mores of the peer group in the conscience of youth. This conflict needs to be talked out together with all of the feelings of guilt it may be causing. Once when a group of us ministers were in the midst of discussing the pastoral care of youth in a clinical training session of a hospital, a group of student nurses happened to enter the room. The leader of the discussion asked if any of them would care to tell the pastors what she thought the pastors ought to know regarding the spiritual needs of youth. Hesitatingly one of them spoke up. "If you could just assure us," she said, "that we don't have to do all the questionable things that our group does—that we can be liked somehow nevertheless—it sure would be a help."

2. *Sex, courtship and marriage.* The Swedish pastoral psychologist, Bergsten, writes, "We need a new sexual morality based on reverence for personality, not in fear of a perfectly natural and necessary function that becomes a curse and a source of sin only through misuse." [1] This is a need not only in Sweden but in many Christian homes and churches in America as well. Youth need the opportunity to accept their sexual nature as a creation of God and essentially good. They need to discuss their conflicts about dating behavior in the acceptive atmosphere of the fellowship of believers, and to know the Christian approach to the goal of it all—marriage and the family.

3. *Family problems.* Youth need religious help to reconcile their natural rebellion against their parents with the

[1] Göte Bergsten, *Pastoral Psychology* (New York: Macmillan Co. 1951), p. 147.

commandment to honor father and mother. They need help in understanding why their parents do as they do, even though they cannot agree.

4. *Religious problems.* Since youth is a time of natural doubting it is imperative that these doubts be faced openly. From their church they need an honest and intellectually respectable apologetic. Along with the facing of doubts there must also be a frank facing of the unanswerable problems. From the emotional side there is the problem of coming to grips with the predicament of recognizing the value of prayer and worship and yet having periodic resistance to doing either.

5. *Vocational problems.* How does one face the future through the cloud of an atomic war threat on the one hand and the pressure of a highly competitive and dollar-conscious society in which success is worshiped on the other? Youth's need for meaning and purpose is the need to see himself as dedicated to God, and his life, a life of service directed ultimately to him.

6. *Problems in living with oneself.* The moodiness that comes for no apparent reason—the inhibiting inferiority feelings that not only cause suffering but sabotage self-fulfillment—the restless agitation that mysteriously plagues youth—all of these need to be viewed in the perspective of faith in God. What are the resources in the Christian message that can help youth cope with these obstacles in relating to himself?

It is in these areas that religion must be applied if it is to have any vital meaning for youth and if youth is to receive the help that he really needs.

A Challenge to the Total Ministry

The pastoral care of youth is a matter of the total ministry as it culminates in the worship and work of the Church.

Although homiletics is a different operational ministry than pastoral care, it is involved in a pastoral way in any total ministry to youth. It is enough to say here that from a pastoral point of view the preacher should expound his text with youth in mind. Surprisingly enough when he does this he may discover that the adults of his congregation are equally benefited. The existential dilemma of youth is not essentially different from the dilemma of his elders, although he meets the dilemma more in the raw and with the intensity of fresh contact.

What has been said about preaching could also be said about teaching. The young people's Sunday-school class is an opportunity to teach the stories and doctrines of the Bible in relation to the drama of life as youth is experiencing it. Although there are usually laymen capable of such an assignment, it is the opinion of some authorities in the field of parish education that if the minister is to teach anywhere in the church school, it should not be the adult Bible class, but the young people's class.

An opportunity for the pastoral care of youth that has tremendous possibilities is the young people's society. In his work with this group the pastor can give his attention fully to youth and their needs. He can help them to plan their program around the vital topics—the problem areas of their life—while still leaving plenty of room for their own initiative in planning and carrying out the program. The strategic part of the program is the guided discussion of these topics. These problem areas represent the felt needs of youth.[2] The Holy Spirit not only speaks to felt needs, but

[2] A recent exhaustive poll of youth and their leaders conducted by the youth departments of several Lutheran bodies, entitled, *Lutheran Youth Research*, not only confirmed that these problem areas represent youth's conscious needs, but also revealed that pastors and other church leaders are amazingly unaware of youth's conscious needs, the implication being that instead of listening to youth they are lecturing.

creates or enlarges the awareness of need. The pastor listens to youth where they are so that he may apply the gospel to where they are living—and listening. The problem area therefore becomes the door through which the gospel becomes meaningful to their lives. Our goal as pastors is not simply to solve the problem, but to make the gospel meaningful.

It is often helpful to break larger groups into smaller units —say ten to twelve in number—for purposes of study and discussion following the presentation of the topic. The aim is involvement on the part of all—having participators and not spectators. People can be involved in a discussion without expressing themselves, but self-expression heightens this involvement and contributes to the stimulation of self-expression of the others. Instead of being content with talks or even answers to questions, let the groups go to work on the topic.

At some youth leadership training schools one night is given over to the question box. The young people write out their questions for a panel of "experts" to answer. At one such occasion a member of the panel suggested turning the questions back to the group to see if it could collectively come up with an answer. We agreed and the first question was, "What can I do when my parents are always fighting?" Soon a youth here and there arose to tell how he or she had dealt with a similar situation in his own home. The suggestions were so honest and helpful and understanding that finally the anonymous questioner arose to thank the group.

I know ministers who include as a sequel to their confirmation or membership training classes a series of meetings in which the class members are stimulated to work together on their common problems in the light of what they have learned. They have found it a very profitable way of concluding their class.[3] Each person stimulates the other, including the group leader, which in these cases, is the pastor.

Instead of focusing on the Christian approach to youth's needs, the program may focus on the study of the Scripture itself. The end result may not be too different since the Christian approach to problems usually leads one into the Scripture and the study of the Scripture usually orients itself around felt needs. The small group discussion method is also an effective way of conducting this Bible study. In my own denomination, we hold biennial youth conventions. Bible study has always been a problem at such conventions because of the sheer physical obstacle of trying to conduct a Bible study for four thousand youth. At the last convention the youth were divided into groups of twenty. Group leaders from among the youth themselves were chosen beforehand. The leaders had their own daily session with the overall Bible study leader in preparation for the Bible study the next day. Each morning the Bible study leader addressed the entire group for fifteen minutes in an attempt to create the atmosphere and stimulate the anticipation for the small group sessions. Following this each group went to its own meeting place, in this instance, rooms on the campus of Cornell University, and together with their youth leader, spent an hour on the study of the lesson for the day. The result was that Bible study which heretofore was the problem child of the convention, was now rated by many of the youth as most valuable.

Much of the success of the group depends on the group leader. As a resource person he must be as well prepared as if he were going to teach. He must be an intelligent listener who knows how to listen to feelings as well as words. He

---

[3] H. Walter Yoder in "Solving Personal Problems in a Church Group" (*Pastoral Psychology* magazine, April, 1955) gives exerpts from several of these sessions in which the tape recorder was used. The trend in problem solving is remarkably demonstrated in this article.

must be able to clarify what is being said and relate the various comments to each other and to the direction in which the discussion is moving—a direction he must sense. He must be able to recognize good insights as well as to avoid corrective tendencies. This is a guided discussion, not talk for talk's sake, even interesting talk. He recognizes the insights directionally and keeps this direction ever before the group. In dealing with the individuals of the group he helps each to be at his best. He tactfully limits the dominating, and with the same deftness, brings out the more withdrawing.

With smaller youth groups, the pastor will be this leader. With larger groups his task is primarily to train the several leaders, who may be selected from the group itself or from among the older young adults of the congregation. When the pastor is a group leader, he must take care that his position of authority does not lead to dominance. Rather by listening carefully to what is being said and restating it in his own words, he clarifies, sums up, and otherwise guides and stimulates the momentum of the group activity. It is often helpful to keep the same groups over a certain period of time. In this way the group grows in its experience of togetherness. Rather than simply grouping, they are relating one to the other and learning experientially the meaning of the fellowship of believers.

The Young People's Society opens the door to another important opportunity for the pastoral care of youth, namely pastoral counseling. After the group has discussed a topic related to these problem areas and the Christian resources for dealing with them, the pastor may say at closing, "Some of you may not be fully satisfied with our discussion and may want to talk personally to me about some of these things. I would be happy to do so. You can ask me any time." The chances are he will not do this very often before he has requests.

In the pastoral counseling relationship the fear, resentment and isolation one feels over his disturbances are reduced as he shares his problem with an empathic pastor. Talking it out helps to alleviate emotional confusion and brings about a reconciliation to the conflicts within. In this intimate setting of pastoral care the disturbed youth may receive the courage to accept the forgiveness of God, not as an abstract dogma, but as an existential experience mediated through the pastor's own acceptance. Personal counseling also gives the pastor an opportunity to give individual help in prayer as he prays for and with these counselees in their problems.

Perhaps as a pastor you feel that you have to start from scratch so far as any ministry to youth is concerned. You have a very ineffective youth group, perhaps none at all, and your pastoral counseling opportunities with youth are few and far between. To start things moving make a check on the names of all the young people within and on the fringe of your pastoral responsibility. Invite them to the parsonage in groups of ten to twenty for an evening of fellowship and discussion. Make the contact personally and arrange the date to the convenience of the group as well as yourself. This helps to insure the maximum attendance. After the preliminary small talk, stimulate them to think together concerning what the Church means or could mean for our day. Get their ideas concerning how a youth group can contribute to the life of the Church and to the lives of its members. Help them to plan together a program for the discussion of Christianity at their interest levels. Encourage the more shy or even shallow youth to make a contribution. Show appreciation for what is said, even though it may fall short of your own ideas or even ideals. You can get much enthusiasm up for the launching of this program because your own enthusiasm is contagious, because the ideas are the group's own ideas, and because through it all the spirit of serving the Highest is apparent, and it is this that appeals most strongly to the natural idealism of youth.

Projects for Service

In addition to planning a program for youth meetings, plan a program for action. Youth have a need not only to receive but to give. "People are sick not only because they have not received love, but also because they are not allowed to give it." [3] All of us have a need to devote ourselves to that which is meaningful and lasting. The youth group can offer to youth the needed opportunity to contribute to the kingdom of God in a way that is tangible and personal. By contributing themselves to that which holds the ultimate meaning to life, they receive meaning for their own lives.

The projects should go beyond money-raising schemes or repairing the roof. As one veteran church worker put it,

There is not one major committee in the church on which I have not served as a member or chairman. Always the relations with my minister were along the lines of church organization. But once—just once before I die—I would like to sit down with my minister and my church friends and think about ways whereby my religion could become a way of life. [4]

The projects should build around the central idea of Christian service, namely, the worship of God and the welfare of people. Naturally there are many such projects and they differ according to the locality. Following are three ideas that have a more or less general application.

1. *Evangelism through the youth group.* The youth of the Church meet the nonchurched youth at school, in the neighborhood, and in community functions. They should be encouraged to make friends with the outsider and to invite him to accompany them to the youth group. The social and entertainment aspects of the group's activity may be the opening wedge here. The group can be instructed and en-

[3] Paul Tillich, *The New Being* (New York: Scribners, 1955), p. 48.
[4] J. L. Casteel, ed., *Spiritual Renewal Through Groups* (New York: Association Press. 1959), p. 30.

couraged concerning the welcoming of new faces. It is also the pastor's opportunity to meet these new young people under the most favorable circumstances.

2. *Youth services in the church.* It is good for both the congregation and the youth to have occasional youth-centered services during the regular Sunday morning worship hour. The idea is not only that youth are talked about, but that youth participate. Even in liturgically centered churches, the young people may participate in the worship service by reading the various Scripture readings for the day, by offering the prayer, and even by giving a short sermonette from the lectern. All of this requires time on the part of the pastor as he coaches them in carrying out their particular role, but it is time that is well spent so far as the future of the Church is concerned.

3. *Visitation of older folks.* The rest homes of the community are full of forgotten older people. The shut-ins in the homes of the congregation are lonely people who live mainly for the visitor from the outside. Amazingly enough older folks like to be called on by the youth, and youth get a real thrill in calling on the older folks. Here past and future are drawn together by ties of mutual respect. Not only do the younger people learn to appreciate both the wisdom and needs of older people, but the older people are helped to feel that the youth are not so estranged from them and their ways as they are prone to believe—that the world has not passed them by. Let the youth group take a personal responsibility for the neglected older people in the community.

The pastoral care of youth involves the total ministry of preaching, teaching, pastoral counseling, and church administration. In his aggressive pursuit of these ministries, the pastor can mean much to the youth of his community. In turn the youth of the community can mean much to the life of the congregation.

chapter IX

A THEOLOGICAL APPROACH
TO MID-LIFE

When we think of the problems of middle life we are likely to think of the *change of life* with its subsequent family problems and emotional breakdowns. These involutional disturbances are precipitated by physical as well as psychic changes that intensify to the point of distortion a crisis period that is indigenous to the change of outlook on life that normally comes upon one as he finds himself well into the second half of an expected life span—from the late thirties into the sixties. We begin our theological approach into the issues involved in this epoch of life by examining this change of outlook, the environmental stimuli that influence it and the spiritual consequences that accompany it, before proceeding into its bizarre manifestations when it is complicated by involutional disturbances.

Time of Spiritual Crisis

No one has presented the spiritual nature of the crises in middle life more emphatically than psychoanalyst Jung when he said, "Among all my patients in the second half of life—that is to say, over thirty-five—there has not been one whose problem in the last resort was not that of finding a religious outlook on life." As one "finds" himself in mid-life —and "discovery" it is since he cannot comprehend how he has come so far so soon—he questions his sense of values and feels less confident of his goals. He may actually perceive that he will not reach his goals and have a difficult time shrugging off his feeling of failure. Nor is failure his only problem. He may even have achieved his goals and discovered that to his chagrin he is still unsatisfied. The beauty he sought has turned to ashes once he has possessed it. The overestimated returns from achievement lead only to disillusion. There was the man who bent all of his energies in the direction of education and looked to the Ph.D. degree as the acme of all goals. After the struggles of two decades he achieved his goal. As he received his diploma he was overcome by the thought that this was simply a piece of paper and that he felt no different after receiving it than before. Alexander the Great wanted to conquer the world. By the time he reached his early thirties he had accomplished his goal. In despair he committed suicide because there were no more worlds to conquer. So goes a popular fallacy. Actually Alexander died of fever in Babylon. After two nights of debauchery he became ill, and in ten days he was dead. But the myth of his suicide persists—perhaps because it is based on good psychological if not historical evidence.

Despite how one fares or does not fare with his ambitions, in the middle years life shortens. If life shortens death closes in. When this reality enters his consciousness the individual is naturally led to re-evaluate his goals. By this time of his life he may also have experienced moments of sorrow in which the shallowness of his previous concerns and interests stand out in sharp relief. This very clarity in the contrast of values places him in the position of "finding a religious outlook on life." In fact the crises of middle life are a test for the caliber of ones religious health. Previously a person may have been able to keep one step ahead of the conflicts that threaten to erupt from within him. As a younger person his future appeared as infinity. His body seemed hardly to notice any wear and tear from the abuse of unhealthy emotional patterns. When he reaches mid-life the increasingly limited future can be very threatening and his physical stamina is no longer able to endure the abuse. This means that conflicts that he formerly could outrun may catch up to him—and now he has less resources with which to face them.

Our religious health is synonymous with the character of our relationship to God. When these conflicts erupt upon us they reveal the character of this relationship—whether it has a legal or evangelical basis. If it has a legal basis the person may have been expending his energies in a guilt-driven conscientiousness. His is the desperate effort to keep his debits balanced by his assets. This sort of barter with God reveals his religious motivations. These motivations are concerned primarily with reconciling God so that he can avoid the punishment he feels he deserves. Behind this appeasement of God is a mental image of God that is most unlovable. The individual would just as soon this God did not exist, but since he cannot eliminate him he must pacify him. His religion is largely self-defense. It has been the repeated history of human experience that if we try by good deeds or religious acts to appease God, ultimately we fail. Whatever we do, it is never enough. Our guilt demands more of us than we are able to fulfill. The result is not only frustration but hostility, and the hostility takes over to become the basis for even greater guilt. Tillich says,

Have you ever noticed how much hostility against God dwells in the depths of the good and honest people, in those who excel in works of charity, in piety and religious zeal. This cannot be otherwise, for one is hostile, consciously or unconsciously, toward those by whom one feels rejected.[1]

In middle life when his faculties for appeasement may become curtailed, the anxiety over this inability to reconcile God may predispose a person to an emotional crisis.

The re-evaluation of goals and interests leads the person in

[1] Paul Tillich, *The New Being* (New York: Scribner's, 1955), p. 20.

mid-life to struggle through the experience of the writer of Ecclesiastes: "Then I considered all that my hands had done and the toil I had spent in doing it, and behold, all was vanity and a striving after wind, and there was nothing to be gained under the sun." (Eccl. 2:11.) The writer of these words is taking the negative outcome of his re-evaluation with an apparent philosophical and cynical detachment, but this same conclusion can also produce great anxiety and a heavy sense of judgment. It is a reoccurrence in mid-life of the anxiety of emptiness and worthlessness of youth. But now one is less able to endure it and when it stirs up additional conflicts that likewise have never been genuinely faced, he may face the possibility of a nervous breakdown. But this same individual finds an affinity for another of Ecclesiastes observations: "He has put eternity into man's mind." Previously he may have paid lip service to eternity as he buried himself in his finite pursuits. Now the finite begins to look painfully finite—and there comes the realization that we can seek here no lasting city, but that we must seek the city which is to come. He is open for the ministry of pastoral care.

Time of Family Crisis

In middle life there is the potential for family crisis even without the familiar disruptions to family life created by the complications of the *change of life*. There is for example the problem of the declining family. The house that was alive with children's spats and adolescent complaining is suddenly quiet—terribly quiet. As one father said,

We finally got our house built. It's what we've always wanted for the family. But now we suddenly realize that we have no family—that in just a couple of years our youngest child will

144

be leaving for college. What will my wife and I do with those four bedrooms?"

When the children are gone father and mother are faced with a readjustment to each other as husband and wife. At this time the wife in particular may experience a loss of purpose, especially if she has centered her life around her children. Sometimes a woman finds her family responsibilities a convenient escape from assuming the responsibility for her own growth as a wife and a person. Regardless of what her motivations may have been, if she has focused all of her interests and concerns upon her children she may have a difficult time establishing any identity when they are gone.

It is during this time also that people may experience disappointment in their children. They had great plans for this one or that one—that she would go to college or that he would succeed his father in the business—but things did not work out as they had planned. Instead of going to college she married before she finished high school. Mother and Father felt it was a mistake, and time has shown they were right. Daughter is most unhappily married. Instead of taking hold in the family business the son has shown neither interest nor ability for it. Although the parents had plenty of signs during their children's adolescence that their plans for them were on shaky ground, there were always those pipe dreams that kept up their spirits. "They will straighten out when they grow up." But what happens to father's and mother's outlook on life if they do not?

Nor is it simply the family involvements that complicate life during this time. Being *without* a family can become the focus for a great deal of inner disturbance. The single person in our culture is made to feel cheated by life. Nor does the Church alleviate this feeling with its family nights, couples clubs, young mothers club, parents classes and similar activities that make the single person wonder if there is any place for him? Well-meaning friends tease away at the sore spot, or try to arrange a match, or simply inquire at regular intervals whether there are any prospects in the offing. Until early mid-life there is always the hope in the single person that he will marry and become "normal." But now these hopes appear as pipe dreams and the anxiety may turn into bitterness. Accentuated by a "marriage and the family" culture, the loneliness of those who remain single is a religious need and presents a religious challenge.

Economic Crisis

During middle life people usually are at their high point· economically and this in itself offers great temptations to a materialistic scale of values. But there are factors in our society that intensify the temptation. Ours is a competitive society in which economic status is a standard of success. It is particularly the man of the family who experiences this pressure. He feels it at work and at home. In the words from one of our popular magazines, "He has to worry all day long about being as 'good a man' as his fellow workers; then he comes home to a wife who saddles him with all the worries she wouldn't have if he were as good a provider as the man next door." No wonder that the average wife in our society can look forward to five years of widowhood. Whether he is promoted or not, the man is under tension. If he is promoted, he feels the resentment of his fellow workers who had hoped for this same promotion. If he fails to be promoted, he feels the judgment that comes when personal worth is based on ascending the ladder.

Nor is he correct when he looks with envy at his rural brother. Here too "the heat is on." It is not only how many bushels to the acre the farmer produces but how many bushels compared to his neighboring farmer. It is the progressive farmer who "goes places." So it means buying more machinery to farm more land to get more money to buy more machinery. And if a man gets too far ahead of his neighbors he feels that same resentment in the atmosphere as his brother in town. In addition he faces the growing menace of "corporation farming" which is causing some to predict that family farm cannot survive without permanent government subsidies.

So great is the pressure of economic competition that in our day of possible annihilation by hydrogen bombs, a University of Michigan survey revealed that so far as people are concerned it is money and not peace that makes them happy and the lack of money and not the fear of war that makes them unhappy.[2] The insecurity that exists in some of our industries does not help the situation. The fear of being laid off—the resentment and bitterness that results when the corporation shows no soul—these are hazards that labor unions can reduce but have not eliminated. Our democracy is threatened at its social level by the erection of the barriers of a labor-management class war created by these economic pressures. Curiously enough it is not money alone that keeps these divisions, but the social status which money seems to imply. Although a change in the financial situation may not immediately alter one's social classification—as labor's salaries are beginning to indicate—it does mark the beginning of a change in this direction and the next generation will experience the results.

Social Pressures

Since the economic pressures are generated by social pressures and social pressures are related to the individual's sense of worth, it is obvious that not only does our society "love the praises of men more than the praises of God" but may even use the institution of God to gain the praises of men. It is important for a person's economic and social security

[2] AP News, June 1, 1960.

that he join the "right" church. The institution which more than any other should cut across class distinctions since its Head is no respecter of persons, finds itself in our twentieth century to be a reflector of the class system in secular society. The desperate exodus to the suburbs upon the part of the respectable denominations is due not only to the fact that the membership is finding it difficult to participate in the church program because of distance, but also to the fact that it relieves them of the problem of whether those within closer proximity to the church should be invited in.

The importance of the social factor in the economic competition makes it mandatory for the man who wishes to rise in the economic world to associate with the right people. His wife feels this same pressure. Their challenge is to gain acceptance into the next social order in the hierarchy of status. *Fortune Magazine's* now famous articles on the young executive's wife emphasized the extremely important role that she must play socially if her husband is to rise on the economic ladder. A top executive writing in another national magazine entitles his article, "Before I Hire Your Husband I Want to Meet You." His first qualification for a good wife was that she be friendly. "She smiles easily and she is pleasant to be with. She has many friends whom she entertains within her means, but she is careful to prevent social activities from interfering with her husband's rest, health and efficiency." [3] She is under pressure to entertain impressively and to hope to *be* entertained in return—to be a gracious hostess as well as a gracious guest. It is not difficult to see how people who are caught up in this competitive momentum must think of others primarily in terms of what these people can do for them in their status seeking and to think of their own role

[3] By R. E. Dumas Milner, *Good Housekeeping*, January, 1956, Vol. 142, No. 1, p. 100.

in terms of making the right impression upon these people even at the expense of being genuine.

Under these economic and social pressures the individual competitor faces the danger of becoming a chronic drinker. In its adolescent attitude toward alcoholic beverages our society overrates their role in the social dynamic. While conducting a spiritual life mission in one of our industrial communities I was confronted with the problems that people face in this area. "What do you do when the couples you run around with insist upon having the bottle at every engagement and you do not care to bring the bottle?"

"Can you not simply say no?" I asked naïvely.

"We can if we want to be called 'squares.' It causes a tension in the group when we don't join in. People just don't like it."

"And I suppose it is important to you to have these people as friends," I continued in my naïveté.

"Well, yes. After all most of them belong to this congregation."

The problems of society become the problems of the congregation. How similar are the social problems of the couples in middle life to those of youth. But the bottle is not only a must when the "set" gets together. It becomes a must also in the office and at the plant. When the competitive demands become severe a drink helps one to relax. A drink helps one to be at his best socially too. Soon the drink becomes a very important item in the day's agenda. It is not coincidental that middle life is the age group of the alcoholic and that the number of women as well as men who are alcoholics is increasing at such an alarming rate that alcoholism has become a national problem. This predisposition to alcohol is abetted by the fact that the sense of values that characterizes our socio-economic world makes the spiritual life an anachronism. This results in the impoverishment of inner resources for strength.

Irrelevancy of the Church

The conflict between the system of values in the social and economic world and those of the Christian religion makes the church irrelevant to people who consciously or unconsciously adopt the mores of our competitive society and become "of the world" as well as *in* it. This is the situation frequently with the nominal church member whom every congregation seems to have in abundance. The conflict itself is probably the reason why he is nominal. The church can be irrelevant also to the active church member. For him the conflict is not yet apparent or else has been repressed. But the results are the same. He is using the church in terms of his social and economic value scales in which all relevancy is confined to finite values. But the majority of people—even our church members—feel the church has little to offer for the concerns of this life. Their ties are nominal not only because for them the church is irrelevant, but because of the uneasiness of conscience the church is still capable of producing within them. They sense the discrepancy between their ambitions in the social and economic world and the self-renunciation they identify with the pious life. They experience guilt over their absorption in the material in contrast to the supposedly otherworldly or spiritual concentration proposed by the Church. Because of the mores of their business procedures and the necessary extension of these mores into their social pursuits, they feel on the outside of a fellowship that appears to be oversimplified if not impractical in its ethics and uninteresting and pale in its sociality.

These people are like a certain gentleman whom we can call Mr. Harding. He came from a strict and pious home, but he himself rarely enters the church. His children are practically grown and he and his wife enjoy their home and spend a great deal of time—including Sunday mornings—in their garden. He has worked himself up the hard way in his business. He enjoys his work and is elated by the social overtures that come now and then from the important people of the community. Harding is an excellent neighbor and the kind of friend who helps out whenever there is need. When you ask him if he is in favor of the Church, his answer is an unqualified yes. His pious home background will never allow him to lose respect for its beliefs. But when you ask him why he does not attend church he says, "Well, I'll tell you. The kind of life that I have to live in business and the kind of life that I would have to live if I took the church seriously do not fit together. Now don't get me wrong—my business practices are not bad—nothing illegal you understand. But I'm in business and I have competitors and there are certain things we have to do to stay in business. No, if I went to church I would be a hypocrite, and I don't want to be that. There are enough of those in the church already without adding one more."

Harding is concerned about another fellowship than the fellowship of believers, namely the fellowship that is advantageous to his own economical and social prestige. He is a refined version of the "status seeker," a friendly "organization man," a *darn nice guy* in a "gray flannel suit." It is the experience of youth extending itself into the social milieu of mid-life—the religious conscience *versus* the support of the peer group. Harding has decided against his conscience, or so he says. Actually he has not. He has simply decided that what he believes the Church would place upon his conscience is for the few and not the many, and he is perfectly content to be among the many. Yet Harding is not as secure as he appears to be. Already he is casting an occasional apprehensive glance into the future and the day of compulsory retirement. There is a conspiracy within all the influences of life to bring about a crisis in this period of life, particularly to those who are looking to the finite to give what the finite cannot give. Not the least of these influences are the physical changes or at least what appears to be the physical changes of the involutional period.

Involutional Disturbances

For the majority of people the involuntional period presents no great problem as they pass through it with little difficulty. For some it is an extremely upsetting experience. What causes the trouble? There are physical changes that take place particularly in the woman, as her menstrual cycle comes to an end. The glandular disturbances have their effect on personality and perhaps there is an accentuated physical counterpart among those who have the severest crisis. Yet there seem to be psychic predispositions also. During the involutional period people tend to become "more so." If a woman has been suspicious of others or had feelings of inadequacy, she is likely to have more of these during menopause. If she has been fortunately able to keep one step ahead of an emotional crisis, in menopause the crisis may catch up to her. It is a time when the sense of failure assumes exaggerated proportions as it antagonizes inferiority feelings and heightens the sense of rejection and resentment. It is hard for the family to understand because often it is the woman who has kept her aggressive tendencies well-hidden who finds it impossible to restrain them during menopause. The crisis is similar to the youth crisis but it is at the other end of life. The individual is being prepared for a new stage of life, only this time it is not the climactic stage of adulthood, but the declining stage of middle life and old age. Glandular changes are in the opposite direction of those in youth. The reluctance to leave the old is greater in the involutional period for it means facing what appears to be the decline ahead. This is especially true in our age of sex emphasis. If her fertility is over, is also her sex appeal?

As these fears build up the woman may begin to feel she

is no longer desired, and become depressed. In her depression she may project her fears onto others and begin to suspicion them of dire things. Her behavior may even appear paranoid. She may openly accuse her children of no longer caring for her and her husband of all manner of inconsiderations, including infidelity. The idea is that since she is no longer attractive he will grow disinterested. The next step is that he has already done so, and is even looking elsewhere. She may continue her withdrawal into herself by withdrawing from the activities of church and community life with which she had been associated.

The crisis for men, called the climacteric, comes about a decade later. Much less attention is given to the male "change of life." Severe symptoms occur less frequently than in the female and are often not recognized as the climacteric when they do appear. The differences are probably due to man's role in nature and in our society. He does not experience the pronounced physical changes that end fertility and his role in society is more diversified and less confining. Rather than becoming accusatory and self-righteous the man who is showing the symptoms of the climacteric is characterized by an extreme anxiety. He may have experienced a temporary loss in his sexual potency and become fearful that he is losing his virility. The anxiety itself would then inhibit his sexual responses—together with other natural functions such as appetite and sleep. But the fear of losing virility is made into an irrational anxiety by the deeper fear it symbolizes—the fear of being a failure as a person. Virility implies life; its decline, death. The approaching of the end and the sense of failure as a person unite to produce the anxiety of judgment and doom. Consciously however the man is far more aware of the pain of anxiety than of any cause or causes. His usual statement is that he does not know what is happening to him except that he seems to be going to pieces. In contrast to his female counterpart he openly asks for help.

The involutional disturbance is a crisis that demands a change in viewpoint. The physical loss, either real or imaginary, symbolizes the approach of an end. As ambitions fade life seems over. Some people in middle life may be able to view death—or life for that matter—realistically without becoming depressed with the shallowness of their goals, but certainly not all. Some too are like William Randolph Hearst who would never allow the word death to be mentioned in his presence. What we need at this time is a faith which is large enough to reconcile these threats of finitude. With such a faith one can die to the self that is in bondage to finite goals so that he can really live. This is the change that the crisis of mid-life demands. New goals are needed with an eternal dimension. It is a time of decided spiritual opportunity.

chapter X

MINISTRY TO THOSE
IN THE MID-LIFE

The pastoral opportunity in the crises of middle life is one of spiritual reintegration. This reintegration is made necessary by the peculiar problems of each new stage in life. The faith that was adequate to the demands of life in a previous era of life may be inadequate for what appear to be the greater demands of the succeeding era. When this inadequacy is experienced there is a spiritual crisis. If the old had been adequate there would be no crisis. But when there is a crisis there must also be a change. The process of change involves the painful experience of reëvaluating everything in one's life. The faith that emerges from the re-evaluation is bound to be a stronger faith than the individual had previously, for the new faith can encounter what the old faith could not. These periodic crises in which the old dies because it is proved inadequate are developmental steps in the process of growth by which all things are becoming new. They provide the pastor with unique opportunities for his ministry.

Doctrinal Opportunities

The crises of middle life among other things are struggles between a religious and secular view of life. Religion is most irrelevant to life in one moment and disturbingly relevant in another. It is in the area of these ideological clashes that people need theological support. Despite the emotional nature of human conflicts our rational natures are also involved. The help that the intellect receives through preaching and teaching to resolve this conflict over values and goals has its transference to the emotions. The doctrinal issues of great existential moment in mid-life are those regarding eternal life, human ambition and material values.

Eternal Life

In our day the idea of eternal life is deëmphasized even in the churches. Theologians like Tillich try to revive it by giving it qualitative rather and quantitative significance, but the qualitative has even less relevance to our secularist culture than the quantitative. The interest in the survival of death is much more indigenous to human nature than an interest in "creating each moment of time into eternity." [1] Even evangelists can largely ignore the issue of death and what follows death.[2] Ours is a this-worldly religion, from the sermons in the pulpit to the home life of the layman. We have here a direct contrast to a former day when religion had a strong otherworldly emphasis which provided a pious escape from the issues of this life. But this-worldly religion can be an escape too—an escape from the question of how or even if the good in life—the kingdom of God—transcends the universal *finis* of death. It is the avoidance of this doctrinal issue in our day that aggravates the natural crisis in mid-life over the significance of life and death.

According to the biblical presentation of eternal life the resurrection of Christ is the assurance that God's Gospel of redemption includes a redemption from the *finis* of death. But this is no mere immortality of the soul or survival of the ego. The Christian doctrine of eternal life is the proclamation of God's victory over all the destructive influences in life including death—a victory in which the individual Christian shall share. In our scientifically minded age it is more difficult than ever before to believe that anything as dynamic as life can come out of anything as inert as death. It is precisely for this reason that the proclaimers of the Christian

[1] Tillich, *op. cit.*, p. 24.
[2] Compare the messages of international evangelist, Alan Walker.

hope must spell out their message where faith has its greatest challenge. Faith needs the inspirational support of the preaching and teaching ministries to meet the particular attacks that are inherent in our present world view.

Actually the otherworldly escapism of a previous religious era was as much of a distortion of the Christian doctrine of eternal life as is our attempt to confine eternal life to the here and now. When the Christian hope is understood as the ultimate and complete victory of God over all his enemies the believer is inspired to greater interest in this life rather than disinterest. His efforts now are insured of ultimate significance, regardless of how futile they seem at the moment. When we work with "eternity in mind," in the final analysis we cannot lose. The here and now is transformed by its eternal significance only because the eternal also has more than a here and now meaning. At the same time the believer is spared the disillusion and corruption of making an idol out of the finite—of living as though these finite concerns of our tangible world—"the things that are seen"—are the "one thing needful." Our pastoral challenge today is to present the Christian doctrine of eternal life in its biblical perspective so that people struggling with their own worth and the worth of their efforts might receive the rational and inspirational help they need to achieve a larger perspective.

Human Ambition

"Flee ambition," said Shakespeare and most of us feel the Bible says the same thing. But how can you flee ambition in a world that rates your value by your accomplishments? The demands upon us are a far cry from a religion that teaches that self-assertion is a form of pride and making yourself small a form of humility. Although many have the impression that this represents the Christian view of humility and because of it have serious problems over their own self-affirmation, the fact is that it is a distorted view of Christian humility. Self-depreciation is a later development and a contrast to the biblical idea. It leads people consciously or subconsciously to sabotage their achievements on the one hand or to feel guilty over the acclaim of success on the other. In the Bible humility is essentially an honesty of personality, a lack of pretense in being more than we are or less than we are. One can be just as proud in making himself small as in making himself big. Consequently a humble person would be devoid of defenses, since he has nothing to hide. Ambition can be a manifestation of pride. On the other hand it can be a manifestation of our God-given creative capacities. Since God is the creative God we who have been created in his image are by our divine endowment creative beings. Taking "pride" in developing this creative potentiality through accomplishments is not the meaning of pride which we understand as the opposite of humility. There is a legitimate desire to do one's best which need not be entirely corrupted by its egocentric distortion to excel over others simply because it is *over others*. In presenting this doctrinal position concerning wholesome ambition the pastor will help free the victims of unnecessary guilt conflicts over their role in our socio-economic society to fulfill their God-given creative destinies. In the words of Paul, "Whatsoever ye do, do it heartily, as unto the Lord." (Col. 5:23.)

Material Values

The great stress on spiritual values in the church and the condemnation of those who emphasize material values gives the impression to many that there is a gulf between the material and the spiritual that the believer had best respect. The idea seems to be that with growing economic stability one desires to possess more *things* in order to add to one's social status and personal comfort. In our culture with its no down payment attractions we do not need much economic security to have most of the latest *things*. Despite the fact that concentration on material things tends to detract from spiritual values, the tendency of the church to separate the material and spiritual into mutually exclusive categories does violence to the historic Christian view of the material. Although it is the extreme concentration on the material side of life that moves the upholders of religion to go to the other extreme and eliminate any spirituality in material values, neither extreme helps people to maintain a Christian point of view when they are part of a culture that is characterized by its material advancement. For the sake of these people—most of whom are in the middle years—the pastor needs to clarify the doctrine of material values so that this material world in which they are inextricably involved can become an asset to their spiritual development.

The Christian view of the material world has its foundation in the Old Testament. In contrast to the Greeks of the west and the Asians of the east the Hebrews believed that the material world was a proper vehicle for the revelation of God. This idea is carried over into the Christian practice of the sacraments in which the material serves to communicate the spiritual. Rather than looking at the material world as an obstruction to spiritual development the Christian looks upon it as God's handiwork. In receiving material blessings he is moved to give thanks to God. In this way he sees through the created thing to the Creator, and the material blessing becomes a means of relating to God through the religious experience of receiving with thanksgiving. As the pastor lays this doctrinal foundation he is helping his people to take their religion with them into their material involvements rather than leaving it at church as though their entrance into the world of material concerns was spiritually irrelevant if not actually enemy territory. In fact the greater involvement in material things during middle life means a larger responsibility of stewardship regarding these material things.

In clarifying these strategic doctrinal issues in his preaching and teaching ministries the pastor gives these people in mid-life a new motivation for their interests and their actions. It is in this stage of life when the nominal church member is most likely to become an active church member. As one such person said, "Why did I have to wait until I was fifty-five years old before I discovered what Christianity can mean to my life!" Through the inspiration that comes from the doctrines of Christianity the crises in mid-life can be resolved into the discovery of the writer of Ecclesiastes:

Behold what I have seen to be good and to be fitting is to eat and drink and find enjoyment in all the toil with which one toils under the sun the few days of his life which God has given him, for this is his lot. Every man also to whom God has given wealth and possessions and power to enjoy them, and to accept his lot and find enjoyment in his toil—this is the gift of God. For he will not much remember the days of his life because God keeps him occupied with joy in his heart. (Eccl. 5:18-20.)

Congregational Opportunities

Christian democracy. The congregation as a fellowship of believers offers the pastor unique resources for his pastoral ministry to those in middle life. The economic competition and status seeking that erects barriers between people in our society and intensifies the emotional problems of mid-life ought to be lacking in a fellowship created by a Christ who humbled himself even unto the death of a cross. As someone has put it, "The ground at the foot of the cross is level." Christ's crucifixion created a democracy of spirit among those who are united to God by it. When this fellowship is hindered by the barriers that mar our secular society the meaning of the cross is lost. The Christ who washed his disciples' feet as a prelude to his self-sacrifice is denied whenever those who claim to be his disciples exalt themselves and attempt to humble others. Nevertheless where a genuine fellowship of believers exists the problems of division created by race and by economic status have their most favorable environment for discussion and solution. The man who feels shut out from the fellowship of others because of his economic or social status should be able to relate to these same people in the fellowship of the Church as an equal. The one thing they have in common—devotion to a Master who though he was rich for our sake became poor—is bigger than the many things that divide them. Here then the sense of self-worth and appreciation from others should be restored.

It is the minister's task to pastor the fellowship group as well as the individual. He is the watchman on the walls of Jerusalem who guards against the entrance into the fellowship of the spirit of the antichrist who would create division and faction. He is the proclaimer of the gospel who never allows the fellowship to deviate from its first love and purpose for existence. Nor does he permit the fellowship to be a mere escape from the divisions of society. It is necessary that he have a pastoral interest in the social problems which beset people and not only face these problems within the discussion of the fellowship but carry this interest into the hotbeds of division within the local community itself. In this way he pastors the fellowship so that it is not merely a retreat from society but a leaven in society.

Talents for the church. In spite of its financial associations stewardship in the Church means more than giving money. Although the original talent in the parable was a piece of money, it was the effort and ingenuity of the servants in increasing the value of the talent that warranted the praise of the master. By the time people reach middle life those who are associated with them have a fair idea of what their particular abilities are. The pastor in his capacity as an administrator is challenged to appraise the talents of his individual members and to plan ways and means in which each may use his interests and skills for the Church. This helps the Church and the member. As a good administrator he should make the request to serve in person. Not only does this help to insure acceptance, but it raises the value of the task in the person's eyes. Many of our jobs in this industrial age do not adapt themselves to the spiritually romanticized Protestant doctrine of glorifying God in your vocation. It may be the extension of the vocation into the avocation in church work which gives it its sense of value and dedication.

Vocational retreats. The church in Germany has made a great contribution to the integration of religion with life in its Evangelical Academies. These academies conduct a regular school year schedule of institutes or work shops in which people from particular vocations gather together under competent leadership to discuss the application of Christianity to their vocation. One week may be for lawyers, another for schoolteachers, another journalists, another salesmen, another industrialists, another leaders of labor. Not all who attend are committed Christians but they are interested to know what the Church has to offer in this field.

My own denomination has attempted to establish similar retreats in this country on the local level through its department of economic life. For example, under the leadership of the director of the department several congregations in an area will send people—usually married couples—representing a predominant vocation in the area—say farming—to a local camp site or other quarters acquired for the retreat for a week end or even for a week. Here they meet to discuss the Christian religion as it relates to their occupation. The division between vocation and religion is dealt with directly so that each individual is moved to make this integration in his own life.

The by-products of such retreats are almost as important as its central objective. The fellowship that develops out of this mutual concern helps the people to realize more than perhaps ever before what it means to relate to one another "in Christ." The times for Bible study and prayer at these retreats are an additional factor in breaking down the division between religion and vocation. For a religious integration of life the "contact" between our spirit and his Spirit must be kept open. This is the gist of the apostolic injunction to "pray without ceasing." But to keep the contact with God open at all times we need to have certain times when we do nothing but concentrate on this contact. Many people realize this need but feel at a loss to establish any such devotional discipline. During the retreats they participate in these devotional practices. In this setting they can see that devotional periods are not something we engage in along with the many other and unrelated things in a day, but that they are times when we communicate with the God whose presence and influence remain with us even after the devotional period is over.

Organizational opportunities. On a smaller scale the retreat idea can be carried out in the programs of the men and women's organizations of the Church and of the adult Bible class in the church school. What more pertinent place in the spiritual development of people can the study programs of these organizations occupy than that they concern themselves with the relationship of the Gospel to the situations in life that absorb their interest and their attention. The membership of these organizations is mostly comprised of those in middle life and under pastoral guidance their programs can be a part of his pastoral care of these people. The following is an example of an agenda for suggested topics for preparation and discussion at the men's meetings.

QUESTIONS FOR DISCUSSION

1. How would you help a man who has become cynical because of life's disappointments?
2. Why is it that some men seem unaffected by the pressure to succeed and seem to have no ambition at all?

3. How may a man's wife influence his attitude toward his work?

4. What role does drinking play—if any--in the way the average man faces the demands made upon him?

5. Does a person need his own private devotions beyond his family devotions?

6. What suggestions can each give the group from his own experience concerning ways and means to vitalize the devotional life?

7. What are the Christian values in life?

8. How far do these values affect the lives of today's man—of today's church member?

9. What problems will automation present to our society in the coming years? Whose responsibility is it to solve these problems? What can the Church do?

10. Can we believe in a "life in the world to come" in our age?

SUGGESTED SERVICE PROJECTS

1. Study the Alcoholics Anonymous Group, local tavern society, the fellowship of lodges. What are men receiving from these fellowships? How can our churchmen's group meet these needs?

2. Sponsor a careers night for the youth of the Church. Present the latest in coming opportunities in atomic energy, thermoelectric power, solar energy and ultra-sonic research. How does Christian higher education fit in?

3. Offer the suggestions to the ladies' society to discuss the topic of helping a husband to cope with the pressures of contemporary life.

4. Sponsor a husbands and wives night to discuss ways and means of maintaining a spiritual perspective in family life.

Pastoral Care in Involutional Disturbances

The pastoral ministry in the common crises of middle life is a help to people in preventing the extremities of involutional disturbances. When these serious disturbances do occur, they come to the pastor's attention usually as family problems. For this reason it is wise pastoral procedure to consider the stage of life of the husband or wife when confronting these family problems. When the husband says—"For twenty years I had the nicest wife a man could ask for. But now! I don't know what's happened. It's hell to live with her. I just don't know how long I can stand it"—the chances are his wife is having a serious menopausal disturbance. Or when the children say—"We don't know whom to believe. They are at each other most of the time anymore. If all the things that Mother says that Dad is doing are true, he is certainly a cad. But we can't help believe that Mother's imagination is working overtime. When we don't take her side against Dad she accuses us of not caring for her at all." When they say regarding their father—"Dad seems to be losing his grip. He can't sleep. He can't concentrate. He cries a lot—says he's a failure. He seems afraid of something but he doesn't seem to know what it is"—the father is probably experiencing a severe climacteric. When people are having involutional disturbances they undergo a period of crisis in which they do not function rationally, and the irrationality of their behavior is of such a disturbing nature that the pastor usually hears about it.

Since it is the family that often bring the problem to his attention the pastor can begin his ministry to the person by helping the family to understand the nature of the trouble. If they realize that wife or mother is undergoing a change of life that has physical and emotional repercussions over which she has little control, they are less likely to react in kind when one of her behavior outbursts takes place. Once they understand what is going on in her life, they will not treat her as one who is responsible for her behavior. They will see that she is in need of help rather than judgment. Medical help is available for these involutional disturbances, and when the family is understanding they are more likely to secure her co-operation in obtaining this help than if they become antagonistic toward her.

If there is a physician in the community who specializes in these problems such as a gynecologist, the pastor should seek a working relationship with him for just such times as these. Not every physician is prepared to cope with the intricacies of this sickness. Some women experience the menopause prematurely. It is even possible that the first symptoms will be psychic rather than physical and a woman may actually be emotionally in menopause while still menstruating. Because of these irregularities the pastor who recognizes the behavior symptoms may be the first to suspect the cause of the problem. In severe disturbances where medical help is not sufficient to curtail the psychotic tendencies, electric shock treatments are highly successful. But in all these opportunities for help it is important to secure this help as soon as possible and the pastor is often the key figure in accomplishing this because of his ministry to the family.

If the pastor follows the principles of pastoral counseling and responds selectively to what the woman herself expresses to him, he may succeed occasionally in getting behind her self-righteous defense and her accusations to the fearful and despairing self. If he responds understandingly at this point she will usually continue to express her sense of inadequacy and failure. Because she feels hurt and worthless she will deeply appreciate the empathy he shows when she bares her soul. At this point he may help her to see the role of her stage in life in the problems she is having. This is a delicate moment and she may become defensive again. Even so when he sows the seed under these favorable conditions it may still grow. Once she is able at times to recognize that her condition is also involved in her disturbances, she is more open to receive medical help and to have moments of genuine reconciliation with her family.

When she has had the satisfaction of expressing her feelings to the pastor, she will be receptive to his ministry of Scripture and prayer. She desperately needs help and may even break down emotionally when he prays with her. Her psychotic tendencies are not stabilized and in her clearer moments she can be helped by pertinent words from the Scripture and the ministry of prayer. When he has her confidence in this way the pastor can encourage her to keep up with her activities, particularly her church activities. It is reassuring to her to hear him say that she is wanted and needed and that he wants her to continue. Her withdrawal is caused by her lack of self-confidence and after she has withdrawn her confidence deteriorates even further. Anything that can be done to keep her involved in outside activities will be a help in preventing this progressive loss in confidence.

Not only is the male climacteric much less likely to create psychic disturbances but even when it does it rarely causes marital problems as does menopause in women, unless the man begins to act out his anxieties in becoming silly around young girls. Usually however he is consciously sick with anxiety and is dependent and appreciative for any attention. The pastoral ministry consists in frequent visitations. Since he is lacking in the paranoid characteristics he is easier to visit. After the pastor has helped him express his fears, he is ready for prayer and Scripture and the reassurance that he *will* come out of this condition—that it is a temporary phase and will pass. He may have to hear this over and again. His suffering is intense and continuous so that frequent reassurance about the final outcome is a great need. In the meantime his suffering can be a stimulus for deepening insight into himself and into the resources of the gospel.

These involutional disturbances often last longer than the crises of youth but they will pass. The main thing is to prevent damage, either to the marriage or the family relationships or the person himself. Rather the pastor may be used of God to convert the whole experience into a means for deeper spiritual understanding and family relating.

chapter XI

A THEOLOGICAL APPROACH
TO OLD AGE

While growing old has always presented its problems, in our day older people have become one of our major social problems. For one thing there are more of them. At the turn of the century there were eleven young people for every one older person. Today there are only four. When we consider that this is also the day of the population explosion so far as the number of young people are concerned, we begin to realize just how many older people there are. There are actually four times as many people sixty-five years and older today as there were sixty years ago. Naturally our medical advance deserves the credit for this. But it is a question whether it is an advance if with the increase in the quantity of life there is brought about a decrease in the quality.

Numbers alone do not account for the problem. With the growing emphasis on compulsory retirement in the mid-sixties there is also an increase in the number of older people who are idle. The urbanization of our culture has created pressure for forced retirements as an apparent means to provide opportunity for younger people. But even on the farm the older person is "forced" into retirement. In a previous generation he continued as long as he was able to farm the family farm and his sons worked for him. Lack of modern farm machinery made it necessary to have several hands. Today the rural society is changing, and the farmer may retire even before his brother in the city because his son is willing to stay on the farm if he can have the farm.

In contrast to growing statistics, there is less room for older folk today than there was sixty years ago. Previously where generations had lived together under one roof, today's rule seems to be that "no house is big enough for two families." For one thing our houses are smaller. For another the increase in machinery has decreased the work. There is no place and no purpose, and in trying to find a place older folks may irritate and threaten those in the home who have a place. Even the quilting that grandmother used to do today has little appreciation.

This change in the status of older people indicates there is less respect for them. They are no longer important in our society. One of our students in clinical pastoral training is from Ethiopia. His particular clinical assignment was in a county nursing home for older people. What I had thought would be a relatively easy clinical experience for him was most disturbing. In Ethiopia the older people are venerated. He approached these county home patients in the same manner as he would an older person in Ethiopia. But the situation of the older people in the home was a contrast to this respect he was showing. Even the older people were confused. What he could not understand was how we in America could push the older people to the side. Even in the best of our situations an older person may have the misfortune of living too long—long enough to feel he is in the way—a problem. Some years ago I became acquainted with a very fine Christian gentleman. At that time he was nearing the end of his working days but was still intensely interested in his job and his family and his church. But then the blows began. First he was demoted at his work on the basis that he needed something a little easier. Next he was retired all together. Then his wife became ill. Finally they sold their home and moved in with a son. After the newness of the move had worn off friction developed between his wife and his daughter-in-law. My friend would have liked to have moved out. But it was too late. Day after day he had to listen to the wrangling. His own body grew more feeble; his interest in life was gone. One day when despair was obviously too much he killed himself.

Days of Decline

The days of old age are days of decline. The body declines. The older person just "can't do" as he used to do. His mental abilities may also decline. He retains his sharpness for past memories, but recent events and new names may slip. Then comes the decline in usefulness. Even if body and mind would allow the older person to continue to be useful, society will not. He must step aside and let the next generation take over. With this comes the decline in being needed. This loss of purpose may accentuate the normal decline of body and mind. There may also be grief over the lost. This is most pronounced when the older person has lost his mate. It is not uncommon that this grief will move the older person to desire and even pray for the experience of talking with the departed. Sometimes they honestly believe they do. While the grief over the lost mate is genuine, it is also symbolic of all that is lost out of this life, including the lost status.

Particularly for those who have lost a mate the result of all these declines is an intense loneliness of spirit. Being set aside by the generation that has the status they once occupied, they feel no rapport with this dominant group. Death with all of its uncertainty can seem more and more desirable in contrast to a life of mere existence. So death for many older people is a hoped for escape—and for that matter, heaven is also. But there are some religious complications to this longing for death and the life beyond. The forsakenness that these people experience from others can be projected also to God. In fact they may also feel forsaken by the Church, which makes the projection to God that much more logical. But we cannot help feeling resentful toward those we believe have forsaken us. When these feelings are toward God, the more pious older person may suffer inwardly in guilt over them. Others may simply grow skeptical and bitter. The result of all this is frustration from which there really seems to be "no exit."

The one escape open is senility. No longer are we under the mistaken notion that senility is something that "just happens" to older people. Much of it is caused by the emotional repercussions of an empty and forsaken existence. At this stage of life people simply cannot take the despair in being set aside.

Old Ben Hale was faced with spending the remainder of his days in a wheel chair in the charity ward of a general hospital. Ben wanted his sons to take him into their homes but they all had reasons for not doing so that satisfied them but not Ben. He sat in grieving and bitter silence. Whenever people visited him he would tell his tale of woe and with tears plead to be taken home with them, insisting he could still work with his hands and be useful.

As a result his family and friends visited him as rarely as possible—with the exception of a theological student who called on him as part of a class assignment. Unfortunately this student became the bridge to senility for Ben. After listening repeatedly to Ben's lament, the student began to encourage Ben to replace reality with fantasy. He called him Dad. After a few months Ben was calling him Son. The student told "Dad" he needed his help to get through his seminary education. He encouraged "Dad" to believe he was actually doing this. Ben responded. He was escaping from despair over being forsaken into being the proud father of a boy who was studying for the ministry and needed his help. Ben had been helped toward happiness but had been led into senility in the process. Our challenge as pastors is to help older people find a purpose for living, not in fantasy but in real life. Not only may senility be indefinitely postponed by purposeful living, but normal and independent living could be restored to thousands of older people through proper treatment and care.

Defects in Our Culture

The tendency of our culture to set older people aside points to an obvious defect in our culture. We worship efficiency and older people are slowing down. We worship physical vigor and the bodies of older people are declining. We worship sexual vitality—the romantic naturalism of Tennessee Williams in which sexual passion is not only the essence of life's meaning but its directing influence, and older people have little of it. We worship youth and old age is its antithesis. We worship production of the assembling line and the production of older people is in a different category.

While living in England we could not help notice the difference between English society and that of America precisely in these areas to which we have been referring. Americans for example have a difficult time understanding the English merchant because he is obviously not governed by the gods of efficiency and production. Frankly this can be irritating at times. Nor is youth the coveted epoch of life. It was middle life that seemed to be the glorious age and the youth whom we knew actually were looking forward to this period. Perhaps it is for this reason that English people in their seventies are still pumping uphill on bicycles. Old age did not seem to be so negatively noticeable. In emphasizing middle life rather than youth the English society with its bodily and mental discipline better prepares its young for the period of middle life. Perhaps for this reason middle life seems to last longer.

If there is one thing in which older people ought to excel it is in the wisdom of experience. But our culture is interested in a different kind of wisdom—a wisdom based on science. We prefer to get our wisdom from the psychologists and sociologists, and one can learn this in a graduate school at a very early age. But are we not confusing knowledge as something assimilated, from wisdom as something evolved out of the uniqueness of human experience? Perhaps it is not coincidental that the culture that extolled wisdom also produced the admonition, "Thou shalt rise up before the hoary head, and honour the face of the old man, and fear thy God: I am the Lord." (Lev. 19:32, K.J.V.)

Where older people have no status in society they cannot accept their own aging. They deprive themselves of the satisfactions that could be theirs in the harvest of life and see it instead as only a prelude to death. Says Dr. Martin Gumpert, one of America's outstanding geriatricians,

By accepting the contributions of old age to human dignity and human wisdom we will remove the curse which now makes an important and prolonged part of our life span a dreaded dark corner of misery. By accepting old age and its peculiar ways of living as an active part of our community, with equal rights and responsible functions, we shall render a good and necessary service to our society as a whole.[1]

The Patronizing Approach

Sick societies like sick people react distortedly to their problems. We realize all too well what we have done to our older people. But instead of solving our problem by helping them to regain their self-respect, we try to solve it by "taking care of them." This is the typical reaction to problems over which one has a guilty conscience. Parents who feel guilty over the harm they believe they have done to their children may try to remedy the situation by "doing things" for these children. As a nation we have done the same thing to the

[1] "Old Age and Productive Loss," *Pastoral Psychology*, Sept. 1954, Vol. 5, No. 46, p. 44.

American Indian. After robbing and cheating him out of his self-respect we thought that by "taking care of him" we could redeem the situation. By making it highly difficult for him to be productive and then giving him charity to keep him going we have only demoralized him further. Solutions such as these are not motivated by love for the wronged as much as by our selfish desire to feel better about things in our conscience.

Now our older people must suffer again because of our guilt over the suffering we caused them. The guiltier we feel the more we insist on serving them—anything but to let them serve. When a parent approaching older age loses his mate the first thing the stricken children insist upon is, "come live with us." Anything but to let them face the loss and adjust to it so that as self-reliant people they can continue to contribute to society. Actually this amounts to a reversal of roles. The children now want to become the parents and make their parents into the children. Many children without being necessarily conscious of the fact would like nothing more than to put their parents into the same subservient position which their parents had previously placed them. How many parents have been persuaded to follow this appeal only to live to regret ever having sold their independence out from under them. Ours is a different age from that of previous years so far as attitudes toward elders are concerned. We are not set up for the generations to live together and when this is done before there is any real necessity for doing so, the deterioration of morale and relationships usually follows. Where there is an absolute need for such a move, it is easier for both parties to accept the situation.

As a society we are following this same patronizing approach to our older people. Our solution seems to be to give older people more benefits. This is fine—they should have benefits. But is this not again the old salve for a conscience guilty over setting these older people aside? The idea now seems to be to "make them comfortable." But if this is our only solution or even our major solution it will do neither society nor our older people any real good. If we indulge them with economic and entertainment benefits we will simply increase their dependency and their passivity. By these indulgences we rob them of the necessity of contributing to others and we rob ourselves of the values we could be receiving from these people if we gave them the encouragement to give. It is more blessed even for older folks to give than to receive.

The Growth Behind the Decline

Fritz Kunkel has a diagram representing the contrast between the natural and the spiritual life. It consists of two cones, the one inverted upon the other. The cone that is rightside up represents the natural life of the human being with its goal in self-preservation. The slant of the cone upward to a point represents the gradual decrease and finally the end of this natural life brought about by time. The inverted cone whose point rests upon the base of the other cone represents the spiritual life "given to us as a seed." As the cone representing the natural life decreases in perimeter, to cone representing the spiritual life increases until it reaches its maximum as the natural life cone comes to its point or ending.

The practical implication is that every loss in the realm of natural life could and should be an adequate gain in the realm of the spirit. Loss of money or reputation, accidents, diseases, death of our friends or relatives, and finally the visible approach of our own death—all these losses should become spiritual gains.[2]

Paul said something very similar in II Cor. 4:16-18.

[2] Kunkel, *op. cit.*, p. 287.

Though our outer nature is wasting away, our inner nature is being renewed every day. For this slight momentary affliction is preparing for us an eternal weight of glory beyond all comparison, because we look not to the things that are seen but to the things which are unseen; for the things that are seen are transcient, but the things that are unseen are eternal.

Old age is a time when the outer nature is wasting away. This is plainly evident—a thing that is seen. But something that is not seen is being renewed every day—going in the opposite direction—a growth hidden in the midst of decline. From the point of view of Christian theology the outer nature that is wasting away is the nature that is born of the flesh, but the inner man who is being renewed day by day is the nature that is born of the Spirit. So one must be born the *second* time to see the kingdom of God. (John 3:3; I Pet. 1:3, 23.) The fact that in the inner nature there is a process going in the opposite direction from the decline and decay evident in the outer nature is an indication in this world of our existence of a life that transcends the limitations imposed by this outer nature. The very loss in the inevitable deterioration in the outer nature can contribute to the wisdom, character, understanding and personality maturity of the inner nature. As the losses continue in the outer nature they can stimulate an appreciation for the more genuine values of life simply because the outer losses remove one from the competitive pressures generated by the spurious values of life. In this way, "when I am weak, then I am strong." For this reason the Christian can "boast of his weaknesses, that the power of Christ may dwell upon him."

This position in no way minimizes the tragedy of decline. The losses sustained in physical and mental vitality that time brings about are essentially the sorrows of this world. Nor do we minimize the finality of death by believing in an eternal life. The infirmities of age and the reality of death are symbols and evidences of the finitude of life. But after we have faced the full force of the tragedy of the slow and certain decline of human existence and the reality of death, we see something else evident in this very life which reverses this whole process of decline unto death and points to a world of reality in, with and beyond the world of change and decay. Inspired by faith in God we call this eternal life.

But growth in the midst of decline is not brought about simply because one is growing older. It is brought about by being the kind of person who can profit in his inner nature from life's experiences. It is not a phenomenon inherent in nature as such. It comes about as the person reaches out from the things that are seen to the things that are not seen—or more accurately, as the Spirit of the world of the things that are not seen reaches out to him. Here is the specific challenge in the pastoral care of the aging. The same experiences in life can produce radically dissimilar results in the people who experience them. The deciding factor of whether these experiences of loss will be gain for the inner man or whether they will be losses here also is the attitude of the individual. It is a matter of his faith.

chapter XII

PASTORAL CARE OF THE AGED

The kind of person one is before old age may indicate the kind of person he will be in old age. It is a wise investment for the future for the young to take seriously the admonition of Ecclesiastes: "Remember now thy Creator in the days of thy youth, while the evil days come not, nor the years draw nigh, when thou shalt say, I have no pleasure in them." (Eccl. 12:1, K.J.V.) Even as the pastor's ministry to young families and adolescents lays the foundation in his premarital guidance, so his previous ministries, particularly his ministry to those in middle life, is preparatory for old age as well. The kind of personality material one brings with him into the next epoch of living is very important in his meeting up to the demands of his epoch. It may be well to elucidate this fact in the educational program of the Church.

But even in old age not all depends upon the past. It may be true that you cannot teach old dogs new tricks but we are ministering to old human beings and not old dogs. It is ironical that at both terminals of human life we are plagued with fatalistic clichés. Not only can you not teach an old dog new tricks but a child's personality becomes fixed by the time he is five years old. One is about as false as the other. Older people can grow. Dr. Robert Golliday, who was an esteemed pastor in Columbus, Ohio, for almost half of a century, died in his eightieth year during which time he was taking a course in philosophy at Ohio State University. There are obstacles in the way of older people's growth. Rigidities of personality may become more rigid in old age and the need for a system of defenses even more desperate. There are also the curtailments on an older person's activity which society imposes. The pastor must reckon with these limitations as they pertain to individual older people, and accept the fact that he may not always be able to accomplish as much as he would like in his pastoral care. At the same time he will continue to try knowing that with God all things are possible. Even though he may have to adjust to the fact that some older people are not going to respond to any appreciable extent, of more importance is the fact that others will.

Helping Older People Serve

From our understanding of the need of older people to continue to contribute of themselves to others, we would expect in our pastoral care of older people to help them to meet this need. This is largely a matter of administrative capacity. Here are people differing in one way from everybody else—they are *not* busy. If there is one thing that they have plenty of it is time. They are also people with a long experience of doing. Some are even open to try new things. It takes imagination and ingenuity to keep these older people involved in the life and work of the Church. But administration and church planning are dependent upon how well the pastor knows his people. No program for older people can substitute for his personal relating to these people. In fact the successful program grows out of this relating.

The fact that older people are potentially valuable to the life and work of the Church does not mean that they are openly asking for a job. Some may even say they want no part of any work. "We've done our share," they say. "Let some of these younger people do the work now." There may even be a little hostility toward the younger people in this remark. The pastor's encouragement may overcome their resistance. "Yes, you've done more than your share in the past. But this is why we want you now. We want you to work along with us. We need your experience. Come along with us in an advisory capacity at least." Many exhibit reluctance because they want the reassurance that they are really wanted. Older people are tired for very obvious reasons. Yet it is necessary that they keep serving in some capacity, for it is the giving of ourselves that brings satisfaction.

The attitude of the pastor toward the older people and their contributions will do much to influence the attitude of the congregation. If he values their role the congregation will grow to value it also. If the pastor and his congregational helpers think together creatively they will realize many opportunities within the local congregation or in the larger church federations for older people to serve. Think of the host of committees that exist in each congregation and in local and regional denominational and interdenominational activities. Each of these committees ought to include at least one older person. In my own denominational social action committee the elderly father of Walter and Victor Reuther served for years as a valuable member and many times wisely influenced our actions simply because of the quality of thinking he had developed through the years. Think of the many young mothers in the congregation or community who are tied down day after day because of small children. In some churches teams of older women and middle-aged women have been organized to give these mothers a break in their day. While older women cannot cope with the strains of little children for any length of time they can if they work together in mutual support occasionally perform this service. It may even be feasible in some communities to organize a day nursery on this basis with different teams of older women making a brief contribution on a weekly or even fortnightly schedule. The good that this service can do for these young mothers as well as their families and their marriage is only matched by the satisfaction that those who give the service receive.

In every church there are tedious sitting jobs. Usually we

beg some busy man or woman in middle life to do them or try to interest the physically vigorous youth to perform them. If the church is prosperous enough it hires this work done. Why not use the older people for these jobs—counting the Sunday offering, stuffing envelopes for mailings, stamping envelopes, keeping record books of various kinds, serving as birthday secretaries, telephoning, mending clothing gathered for relief purposes, repairing church equipment, and the like. In the Kiwanis Club of which I am a member our secretary is not an already overworked businessman but a retired schoolteacher whose satisfaction in doing the work is as obvious as the care and concern with which he is doing it.

Group Activity

Generally speaking most churches are organized enough already without adding another organization for older people. The groups that are already organized such as the men's and women's organization or the adult Bible class are enriched by the mingling together of the various age groups in the fellowship of believers. Older people have their place and value in these organizations and every effort should be maintained to see to it that they continue to participate. Yet the growing numbers of unoccupied older people in certain larger congregations may make it advisable for the pastor to consider adding one more group. It would simply be a realistic recognition of a change that has taken place in our social structure and the church must keep abreast. In these instances the existing organizations cannot do justice to the numbers or the needs of these older people without overbalancing their program. Not all older people need any special group activity or any special help at all. Men like Senator Green or Herbert Hoover or J. C. Penney or women like Grandma Moses or Eleanor Roosevelt may be older but they are anything but unoccupied. Some retire but after awhile get tired of idleness and take on new jobs such as the retired government worker who became civilian defense chairman of his state. But not many older people have either the background or the present opportunity to continue indefinitely in a vocational involvement. When a particular congregation has several older people—especially widows and widowers whose place in the social life has been disrupted by the loss of the mate—who feel out of things because they are old, but are still able physically and mentally to do things, the pastor and congregational leaders may help these people by giving them the opportunity and encouragement to form their own church group. If this is decided upon the pastor or a gifted layman should be the organizer. In those churches where there are professional parish workers or group workers or even associate pastors, the group for older people would offer such an associate a fine opportunity for creative work.

The invitation to form the group should be selective rather than general. Older people are usually not going to respond to a general invitation printed in the church bulletin. As empty or as lonesome as they may feel, they will rarely have the zest to take the initiative in a society such as ours. But if the pastor or whoever is in charge makes a special call upon these needy older people and not only personally invites them to a planning session but waxes enthusiastic about the whole idea and encourages them to attend, he will persuade the majority. It is important that the adviser be a person who encourages others to do and does not have the compulsion to do for them. Older people are like younger people—they lose interest in anything that is simply handed to them in which they have had no part in the planning. If it is to be their group, the ideas regarding the structure of the group and its projects and its program must be their ideas. Naturally the adviser can offer suggestions, but without coercion to accept them. In the planning session his goal is to see how many ideas he can collect from the group itself in discussion. As soon as the group is structured sufficiently to have its own leadership, the adviser's roll recedes even more into the background.

The chief feature of such a group for older people is the life in common which they can share and around which they can structure their fellowship. Normally this structure consists of education, recreation and projects. A systematic Bible study is a favorite in the educational part. Or they may discuss such subjects as the Christian approach to specific political and social issues, geriatrics problems, and even international relations. Education in the actual work of the Church in home and foreign missions, social welfare, overseas relief, and ecumenical participation not only is interesting but easy to program. In our day of ecclesiastical executive secretaries each department of the church has its abundance in filmstrips, movies, and literature that is readily available. They help to increase our appreciation of the work our church is doing and to increase our concern for the expansion of God's kingdom.

For recreation the forms of entertainment in which the people themselves participate are more successful than those in which they are passive recipients. The games or other recreational vehicles are important only as means of intensifying the fellowship in its lighter mood. Simply to chat over a cup of coffee is recreational. Picnics in the summer and potluck suppers in the winter add to this atmosphere for chatting. Recreation is also involved in the participation as a fellowship in the education and project areas of the group. The projects in which an older people's church group could adopt would include many of those activities which we discussed in the section on helping older people serve. These activities become more meaningful to the older person when he is part of a group of other people who are at work on the project together. The group provides the needed support for a shaky initiative.

In addition to the activities already mentioned there are two in particular that have proved successful with older peoples groups, namely, drama and calling. Acting remains as fascinating to older people as to others and being old presents no formidable obstacle. If the play includes parts impossible for an older person to play, these can always be filled by others in the congregation drafted for this purpose. Bible stories are the most adaptable not only because they are familiar but because they are in harmony with the purpose of a church group. There are also other plays available for such groups which denominational headquarters or local mental health societies can supply. One in particular is *The Room Upstairs* which deals directly with the problems that are created when an older person lives with his children. In calling upon others older people profit from the mutual support in confidence that the group provides. They are particularly helpful in calling upon their own fellow oldsters who are confined to their homes or in rest homes. But they can also call upon prospective and inactive members with no mean results.

It is striking how similar in structure and function an older people's group is to the young people's society. Both groups need the counsel of others but need also to be self-governing. Both older and younger people need the support of a group to do things on their own and find in the group a real source for morale. In both cases the group can become the major interest in life. Perhaps it is for this reason that an older people's group can be as productive for the life of a congregation as an active and dynamic youth group.

In most instances there are not as yet enough older people in the local congregation who are in need of a special group to make the venture advisable. There are however enough in the community as a whole. Therefore the most practical approach to this problem in many areas is for the churches to go together through their local council of churches or ministerial groups to form an interchurch older people's group. The same procedure for organization would be followed as with the local congregation except that each local pastor would have to work together with the appointed adviser in order to stir up the needed interest among his own people. In some areas the community itself has taken on this responsibility in its golden age and senior citizen societies. When this is not the case it is the churches' responsibility to act. However it is no cause for lament when the churches or church welfare societies must do this job rather than the community as a whole. There are those things that the church is uniquely fitted to do by its very nature. I personally believe that the ministry to older people is one of these. This is because the problems of older people are not only social but religious. We cannot expect the community to incorporate Bible study in its golden age group educational program. Yet Bible study meets a need in older people that secular educational activities cannot. Nor can we expect religious drama from the community group. Yet the satisfaction of dramatizing the Word of God is far greater for the church-related older person than putting on a play simply because it is entertaining.

Anybody who has been associated with these senior citizen groups knows the enthusiasm that they can create in older people. One's first reaction is that this is a patronizing attempt to create a make believe world for older people where the learning of a hobby is supposed to put meaning back into life. But if they are given the opportunities to use their own initiative in these groups, the change in their morale—particularly among widows and widowers—is enough to convince the skeptic. Where it is a community-wide project local avenues of communication may be provided for the group's activities. For example in Youngstown, Ohio, where the Lutheran Service Society sponsors a very successful community group the local television studio has on occasion given the time for the group's dramatization of Bible stories.

There is one other advantage in a church sponsored group. The ties of appreciation and gratitude that the group develops within the older participant are then directed to the church. The fellowship of the group is directly related to the fellowship of believers and the meaning of the Church and its gospel is clarified by the group experience. This greater appreciation of the Church which the group creates is important not for the Church as one competitive institution in society among others but for the welfare of the older person himself. Dr. C. Ward Crampton whom many of us recall with affection as the helpful writer on physical fitness in *Boy's Life* magazine during our youth is now a distinguished geriatric specialist. He has devised a five-point program for the life enrichment of older people for the YMCA. The fifth point is "Praise God." If praising God is indispensable for the life enrichment of older people it is imperative that the Church of God be the agency in society that is seeking his betterment.

Visitation

The ministry to older people through visitation is the primary ministry to the shut-in. The pastoral call upon the shut-in is an important event in his life, perhaps the most important. Therefore the calls should be made as frequently as the pastor's time budget allows—say once in two weeks—and with some degree of regularity. This helps the shut-in to know about when to expect the pastor so that he has something to count on and to look forward to. The pastor should have privacy in his visit with the shut-in. Sometimes the members of the family with whom the older person is living will stay in the room and more or less govern the conversation. Perhaps they feel this is their hospitable duty.

More than likely they want to make sure the older person does not complain too much to the pastor. It is necessary that the pastor structure the situation from the beginning and explain that he would like to be with the older person alone. Although there may be an awkward pause the relative will abide by the pastor's wishes and in time accept them. Naturally the shut-in may complain. His lot is difficult. If he can release his negative feelings to the pastor he will feel better for it. He will also be easier to get along with for a season. Therefore it is actually to the daughter's or the son's advantage to give the older person the privacy with the pastor to say what he wills. Perhaps the pastor can assure them that he understands the discontent that overtakes a shut-in at times and is not going to take every complaint at its face value.

The pastoral call upon the shut-in may become an opportunity for pastoral counseling. When this is the case the pastor should follow the same pastoral counseling principles as he would with anybody else. One area most likely to call for counseling is the grief these people experience over the lost. Whether it is the lost mate, the lost status or the lost ability to get about, the pastor should hear him out and respond to the feelings that are being expressed. This is the therapy for grief and with older people it may have to be repeated over and over. By allowing him to share in this way the pastor will gain the shut-in's confidence which he may use to encourage the person to work himself back into a meaningful way of life to the extent that this is possible. Some older people are so rigidly defensive and negative that the pastor soon realizes that response to a pastoral counseling ministry is unlikely. He can still visit profitably with these people and depend upon his closing devotions and his administration of the Lord's Supper to give them the spiritual support they need.

Because of the great need of the shut-in for visits from

the outside to break up his day, the use of laymen for visitation is a helpful supplement to the pastoral visits. We have already mentioned the use of young people for this purpose as well as other active older people. However the majority of the callers are usually people in middle life whose family responsibilities are coming to a close. It is important that these callers have instruction for their task and that the program itself be supervised so that records are kept concerning the time and number of visits with each shut-in together with any pertinent information about the call that should be known. A competent layman could easily function in this supervisory capacity.

Beside paying a visit upon these people in the name of the church these callers can also offer home services for the church. The United Lutheran Church for example prints a weekly church service corresponding to the church service conducted on that Sunday together with a brief sermonette. The weekly lay caller could deliver something like this that keeps the shut-in involved in the worship life of the congregation. Some congregations tape the morning service or at least the sermon and distribute the tape to the shut-ins. In addition to having the experience of the visit the shut-in is helped by the use of the tape to join in spirit with the activity of the fellowship. He also is helped spiritually by the content of the service and sermon. It is usually unnecessary for the caller to remain through the playing of the tape. A system can readily be worked out among the callers for pick-up and delivery. Special recognition should be given to the shut-in on his birthday and on the church festival days. Beside the special visit the fellowship as a whole can be encouraged to remember these folks by cards at these times. Older people love to receive cards because they are evidences that they are not forgotten or forsaken.

There may be other older people in the congregation who are able to get about but who are finding it increasingly difficult to maintain themselves in their own homes. For these people the congregation can render home service of a practical nature. Volunteers can take turns delivering a couple of hot meals a week to these folks. The thing older people are most likely to neglect when they live alone is an adequate diet and this has its obvious effect on their health. If teams of women from the various organizations would on occasion give these older people—particularly widowers —a hand in cleaning up the house it would be another fine service. When older people live with their relatives the congregation can help out here too. These relatives are often tied down with these older people. They need times to get away from their vigil of care. The members of the congregation can see to it that they have these times. Transportation is a big problem for older people. Normally they no longer maintain an automobile, bus service is encreasingly inconvenient, and taxis increasingly expensive. Car service can be arranged for these older people so that they can attend as many of the functions of the congregation and community as possible.

The Church's Long-Range Program

At the present time the Church is attempting to meet the needs of its older people primarily by establishing homes for older people. This is the most expensive kind of program and benefits the smallest number of people. Among the relatively few older people that these homes contain, many could have continued on in their own with some assistance. This is evident from the fact that many of these homes will accept only the healthier older folks who can for the most part care for themselves. Some denominations such as the Methodists have established rather elegant homes with private cottages or apartments. Naturally these are ideal but they are primarily for those who can afford to pay for these facilities and even with this limitation these homes have large waiting lists.

Many church operated homes are primarily custodial in service and this is not enough. While the rooms may be pleasantly painted and well furnished and the food carefully planned, older people need more than to be physically comfortable. Otherwise they will rock and walk and wait for the next meal, for bed, actually for death. The dullness of the days and the longness of the nights are a fertile setting for friction and petty complaining. In the words of Margaret Frakes whose excellent study on older people for *The Christian Century* did much to awaken the Church—"A home should be designed . . . so people can be helped not only to live but with God's help to come to life." Our primary responsibility in these homes is to involve these older people in creative activity. In addition to custodial service our homes need a well-planned program involving cultural and occupational opportunities. Because of the many financial arrangements and property settlements that confront older people as they enter a home, they should have competent counseling opportunities. Even more than when they were on their own they need an adequate program of pastoral care. Since we are woefully lacking in personnel for our institutions who are educated for these tasks, we could pioneer in our church colleges in a vocational curriculum in the care of the aged.

The most pressing need for homes for the aged are for those who can accommodate the infirm who are either bedfast or for other physical or mental reasons can no longer care for themselves even with assistance. It costs more money for this type of institution and requires more personnel. Again the local congregations could assist with volunteers— congregational "gray ladies"—who can help out in these homes by working individually with the patient so that interest in life can go on.

There are other services beside establishing homes for the aged that the Church could provide. A very successful experiment in the care of the aged is the day home where older people can come for the day and participate in the social, cultural and creative oportunities of the program and then *go home* for the evening. This provides for the needs of the older person without taking away his independence which is symbolized by his own home. It also helps the living conditions in the home where the older person is living with relatives. Another service is the case worker who can visit the homes of older people and especially the homes where older people are living with relatives and offer assistance and counsel in the various problems and needs evident in such situations. A local council of churches could hire such a trained worker to serve the congregations.

Often pastors are in a position to give advice at critical times in the lives of older people. Generally speaking it is best for older people to continue to live in their own homes and retain their independence as long as this is possible. Giving this advice in due season may prevent some hasty and unwise decisions. With our growing awareness of ways and means for assisting older people in their homes we can help them retain their self-reliance and their place in society for a longer period of time than we would normally expect. There is a growing tendency to find foster homes for older people in which they can live with a family other than their relatives. While this is still in the experimental stage the pastor is in a key position to assist social agencies or even individual older people in locating these homes among his own parishioners.

As the pastor and the local congregation work together with councils of churches and community organizations they can exert influence in the shaping of our societal patterns. We are in need today for a more humane approach to retirement. There is a happy medium between letting a person work indefinitely and cutting him off indiscriminately at a certain age. Individuals differ even in their rate of aging. Retirement rules are needed but not the kind that make no provision for the capable older person. So long as a person is able to do his work he should be allowed to continue in some capacity to do so on a yearly basis so that when he is no longer able both he and the firm are protected.

On the local and national level the Christian congregation can exert its influence to hold the balance between the extremists who would solve all older people's problems by more legislative benefits, some of them economically fantastic, and the self-made man who thinks every older person should be as self-reliant as he is. There are good points in the welfare state and in the rugged individualism of free enterprise and we need to preserve them both. With our rise in the cost of living older people should have more benefits particularly in the area of medicine. They also need a place in society to serve. Interest and enthusiasm produce physical and mental vitality. Giving them a place of respect in which they can contribute of themselves is a stronger stimulus for better health than legislative benefits even for medical aid.

CONCLUSION

Our purpose has been to present the theology and practice of pastoral care as they relate to the natural epochs in the development of the human being as these are experienced in family living. With this goal in mind we have concentrated in the areas of marriage, parenthood, youth, middle life, and old age. How shall we evaluate this approach? Certainly it has its limitations. Problems stemming from other bases of operation than the life cycle of the family may still influence family living. Chief among these would be problems centering in personality disorders such as neuroticism, sex problems per se, problems oriented in the culture in which we live, and problems arising from the pastor's own need for pastoral care.

In spite of this limitation the life cycle approach has the advantage of relating pastoral care to the parish pastor rather than to the specialist pastor. As the parish pastor is relating to people in the whole gamut of the life cycle, it is helpful for him to be alerted to the kind of problems to expect within each stage. Through his knowledge he can recognize the symptoms and interpret the symbols of these specific stages. He can also help others to cope with these problems as they occur in family living.

These stages of life are actually ventures in living that are part of the pattern for growth described by Paul when he contrasts the inner man who is being renewed day by day with the outer man who is decaying. The inner man is being renewed day by day because he is begotten of the second birth, not of corruptible seed as is the outer man, but "of incorruptible, by the word of God which liveth and abideth forever." As the minister of the Word of God the pastor is challenged to apply it where people are experiencing their needs.

More than any other profession that ministers to people in their various needs, the pastor works within the family framework. Because he is the pastor of the congregation he is a part of family and community life. Of all the professions, his alone may join in the family circle. Not only does he know the history and the environment of the people and the community, he shares in them. The family which is a unit in our society is a unit in the Church. In fact the family atmosphere may be the decisive influence so far as Christian nurture is concerned. Its potential for the stimulation of growth and development is unlimited, as its positive ties provide encouragement, confidence, security—in fact all of the values described in the Scriptures as the "fruit of the Spirit."

The close ties of the Church and its ministry to the family unit are further illustrated in the administration of the sacraments. In baptism—specifically child baptism—the reception of the child into the kingdom of God is inseparable from its reception into the family of God. Though it is the child's family that brings the child to the congregation, it is the congregation that commits the child to the family for Christian nurture. In providing the Church a tie not only with the child but with the family, baptism is at the center of the close association of the gospel with the family unit and of the family unit with the congregation. Its administration is an illustration of the family-centered emphasis of the pastoral ministry. Those churches not practicing child baptism have a similar family structure in their child dedication rites.

As a communion between Christ and his Church the sacrament of the Lord's Supper has a direct application to the marriage relationship. Structured according to this same relationship of Christ and his Church, the marital ties are strengthened as the partners partake of the sacramental expression of this relationship. The communion in the sacrament is not simply the vertical communion with Christ but the horizontal communion with our fellow believers in Christ. "For we being many are one bread, and one body: for we are all partakers of one bread." Since communion with Christ is also a communion with our fellow partakers, its role is that of strengthening the fellowship of believers. If this is true for the larger family unit, it is true also for the smaller units.

From the perspectives of both the Church and the social sciences the family atmosphere of interpersonal relationships is a powerful influence for the development of healthy or sick souls. We have noted its positive contributions. There is, however, also the negative side. The family atmosphere can be a basis for that corrupting influence known as conditional love. In their egocentric ignorance parents may actually hinder the development of a self-image in their child, so that the child grows into adulthood lacking in a sense of personal identification and worth.

Due to family deficiencies such as these, individuals find themselves unable to receive from God. Having projected onto him the conditional and whimsical nature of their parents' "love," they find it extremely difficult to trust in God. Because they automatically project these distortions into every interpersonal situation, their religious life as well as their potential as future mates and parents are the victims. Here in the family is also a source of the tragic in life.

In applying the gospel in a pastoral way to the specific needs inherent in these human epochs the pastor will help people to grow in their own development and in the development of their family ties. There is a mutuality here that the pastor must not overlook. Even as the life of the family is influenced by the life stages of its members, so these stages of life are dependent upon family relationships for their whole-some potential. This same mutuality exists between the self in its own development and the development of its dialogue with others. It extends also to our relationship with God. Although the mutuality of these ties represents a total picture it can be viewed from the three angles of God, self and others.

In discussing pastoral care from the perspective of the life cycle in family living it has not been our procedure simply to present directives and techniques, but to explore into the background for such directives by approaching each of these specific areas theologically. Not only is there mutuality and interdependence between theory and practice, but in its theological orientation we have the basis for the distinct nature of the pastoral ministry. Grounded in theology, it incorporates within this perspective the wisdom from the sciences of human relating in its specific ministries of preaching, teaching, pastoral counseling, pastoral visitation, group work and church administration and planning. Through these means the pastor plays an important role in the life of the family. His pastoral reflections and theological integration in the area of family living meet the current need for such reflection and integration at its most vital point. By these efforts the data from the sciences are made to serve redemption's cause. Since it is a Christian assumption that the gospel is the integrating factor of life, the integration of the data of science is not only an example of the gospel's integrating potential but is an integration that is of great pastoral significance. In Christ—consequently in Christian experience—the kingdom of nature (science) and the kingdom of grace (revelation) are made one.

Pastoral care is not something unrelated to theology, or simply biblical or systematic theology applied. It has its own deposit—*pastoral* theology. This deposit points to the pastor's unique role in ministering to the needs of people. The pastor is a member of a team of professional people who is unapologetically different. Through his knowledge of Christ and his integration into this knowledge of the data of the social sciences and his reflections on the pastoral function, he has his own basis of operation—pastoral theology. The needs of people are too complex to be relegated to the services of any one professional person; the facets of human existence form too much of a unity for God to work through one team member alone, even if he is the pastor.

The perspective of the family-life cycle has the value of providing a wider approach to pastoral care than simply a ministry to individuals, as would be largely the case, for example, were our perspective in the area of personality disorders. This broader approach takes us beyond the specific ministry of pastoral counseling to the general practice of pastoral care. The new insights from the sciences are not directed solely to the ministry to individuals or even to specialized group work such as group therapy. Rather they are applicable to the general activities of the working pastor, and as such they serve to deepen his total ministry. By incorporating pastoral counseling and group dynamics into the total role of the pastor, the life cycle approach serves to unify the pastoral ministry. Instead of hanging by themselves as current fads or personal hobbies or specialties, these new movements and functions in pastoral care are seen in their relationship to the total concept of pastoral care and pastoral theology.

The perspective of the family-life cycle leads us away from the individualism often associated with pastoral counseling and personal evangelism. It helps us not only to *see* the individual in terms of his meaningful relationships but to minister to him *in* these relationships. It leads us away from the isolation of individual problems to the stage in the life cycle in which the problem has its specific meaning. By providing us with this wider setting within which to view specific difficulties, our approach helps the indvidual to see his peculiar problems in terms of their normality as well as their abnormality. It is a perspective that is commensurate with the view that the human being is a whole in spite of his parts, and that the human life is a unity in spite of its diverse activities. Biology and spirit are as mutual in their interdependence as are the individual and his family.

Bibliography

Pastoral Theology and Pastoral Care

Hiltner, Seward. *Preface to Pastoral Theology*. Nashville: Abingdon Press, 1958.

Hofmann, Hans (ed.). *Making the Ministry Relevant*. New York: Charles Scribner's Sons, 1960.

Hulme, William E. *How to Start Counseling*. Nashville: Abingdon Press, 1955.

Johnson, Paul E. *Psychology of Pastoral Care*. Nashville: Abingdon Press, 1953.

Oates, Wayne. *Where to Go for Help*. Philadelphia: The Westminster Press, 1957.

Schnucker, Calvin. *How to Plan a Rural Church Program*. Philadelphia: The Westminster Press, 1954.

Smart, James D. *Rebirth of the Ministry*. Philadelphia: The Westminster Press, 1960.

Wynn, J. C. *Pastoral Ministry to Families*. Philadelphia: The Westminster Press, 1957.

Pastoral Approach to Marriage

Bertocci, Peter. *The Human Venture in Sex, Love and Marriage*. New York: Association Press, 1949.

Bowman, H. A. *A Christian Interpreation of Marriage*. Philadelphia: Westminster Press, 1959.

Duvall, Evelyn M. and Hill, Reuben H. *When You Marry*. New York: Association Press, 1956.

Feucht, O. E. (ed.). *Sex and the Church*. St. Louis: Concordia Publishing House, 1961.

Landis, Judson T. and Landis, Mary G. *Personal Adjustment: Marriage and Family Living*. New York: Prentice-Hall, Inc., 1955.

Magoun, Alexander. *Love and Marriage*. New York: Harper and Brothers, 1948.

Morgan, William H. and Morgan, Mildred I. *Thinking Together about Marriage and Family*. New York: Association Press, 1955.

Piper, Otto. *The Biblical View of Sex and Marriage*. New York: Charles Scribner's Sons, 1960.

Rehwinkel, Alfred. *Planned Parenthood*. St. Louis: Concordia Publishing House, 1960.

Premarital Guidance

Adams, Theodore. *Making Your Marriage Succeed*. New York: Harper and Brothers, 1953.

Bovet, Theodore. *A Handbook to Marriage and Marriage Guidance*, London: Longman's Green and Co., 1958.

Burkhart, Roy. *The Secret of a Happy Marriage*. New York: Harper and Brothers, 1949.

The Cana Conference. Chicago: The Cana Conference, 1950.

Duvall, Evelyn M. *In-Laws: Pro and Con*. New York: Association Press, 1954.

Duvall, Sylvanus. *Before You Marry*. New York: Association Press. 1959.

Geiseman, O. A. *Make Yours a Happy Marriage*. St. Louis: Concordia Publishing House, 1946.

Hine, James R. *Grounds for Marriage*. Champaign, Illinois: McKinley Foundation, 1957.

Lewin, S. A. and Gilmore, J. *Sex Without Fear*. New York: Medical Research Press, 1950.

Mace, David. *Success in Marriage*. Nashville: Abingdon Press, 1958.

––––––. *Whom God Hath Joined*. Philadelphia: The Westminster Press, 1953.

Morris, J. K. *Premarital Counseling*. New York: Prentice-Hall Inc., 1960.

Westberg, Granger. *Premarital Counseling*. New York: National Council of Churches, 1958.

Wood, L. F. and Dickinson, R. L. *Harmony in Marriage*, 2nd ed. New York: Round Table Press, 1949.

Marital Crisis Counseling

Clinebell, Howard J. *Understanding and Counseling the Alcoholic*. Nashville: Abingdon Press, 1956.

Earle, Clifford J. *How to Help an Alcoholic*. Philadelphia: The Westminster Press, 1952.

Hine, James R. *Alternative to Divorce*. Champaign, Ill.: McKinley Foundation, 1957.

Mudd, Emily H. *The Practice of Marriage Counseling*. New York: Association Press, 1951.

Stewart, Charles W. *The Minister as Marriage Counselor*. Nashville: Abingdon Press, 1961.

Vincent, Clark E. (ed.). *Readings in Marriage Counseling*. New York: Thomas Y. Crowell, 1957.

Pastoral Approach to the Family and Family Problems

Amstutz, H. Clair. *Growing Up to Love*. Scottsdale, Pa.: Herald Press, 1956.

Baruch, Dorothy. *New Ways in Discipline*. New York: McGraw-Hill Book Co., Inc., 1949.

———. *One Little Boy*. New York: Julian Press, Inc., 1952.

Beecher, Marguerite and Beecher, Willard. *Parents on the Run*. New York: Julian Press, Inc., 1959.

Chaplin, Dora. *Children and Religion*. New York: Charles Scribner's Sons, 1948.

Eckert, R. C. *Sex Attitudes in the Home*. New York: Association Press, 1956.

Feucht, O. E. (ed.). *Helping Families Through the Church*. St. Louis: Concordia Publishing House, 1957.

Prenter, Regin. *Spiritus Creator*. Philadelphia: Muhlenberg Press, 1953.

Southard, Samuel. *The Family and Mental Illness*. Philadelphia: The Westminster Press, 1957.

Trueblood, Elton and Trueblood, Pauline. *Recovery of Family Life*. New York: Harper and Brothers, 1953.

Winter, Gibson. *Love and Conflict*. Garden City, N.Y.: Doubleday and Co., Inc., 1958.

Wynn, J. C. *How Christian Parents Face Family Problems*. Philadelphia: The Westminster Press, 1955.

———. *Sermons on Marriage and Family Life*. Nashville: Abingdon Press, 1956.

——— and Fairchild, R. W. *Families in the Church: a Protestant Survey*. New York: Association Press, 1961.

Pastoral Approach to Youth and Youth Problems

Casteel, John L. *Renewal in Retreats*. New York: Association Press, 1959.

Hulme, William E. *Face Your Life with Confidence*. New York: Prentice-Hall Inc., 1953.

———. *God Sex and Youth*. New York: Prentice-Hall Inc., 1959.

Jersild, A. T. *The Psychology of Adolescence*. New York: The Macmillan Co., 1957.

Myers, C. Kilmer. *Light the Dark Streets*. Greenwich, Conn.: The Seabury Press, 1957.

Nelson, J. O. *Young Laymen—Young Church*. New York: Association Press, 1948.

Wittenberg, R. M. *Art of Group Discipline*. New York: Association Press, 1951.

Pastoral Approach to Mid-Life and the Problems of Mid-life

Brunner, Emil. *The Eternal Hope*. Philadelphia: The Westminster Press, 1954.

Casteel, John L. (ed.). *Spiritual Renewal Through Personal Groups*. New York: Association Press, 1957.

Crowe, Charles M. *Getting Ready for Tomorrow*. Nashville: Abingdon Press, 1959.

Cullman, Oscar. *Immortality of the Soul or Resurrection of the Dead?* New York: The Macmillan Co., 1958.

Heiges, Donald. *The Christian's Calling*. Philadelphia: Muhlenberg Press, 1958.

Howe, Reuel. *The Creative Years*. Greenwich, Conn.: The Seabury Press, Inc., 1958.

————. *Man's Need and God's Action*. Greenwich, Conn.: The Seabury Press, Inc., 1953.

Klausler, Alfred P. *Christ and Your Job*. St. Louis: Concordia Publishing House, 1957.

Polatin, Philip and Philtine, Ellen C. *The Well-Adjusted Personality*. New York: J. B. Lippincott Co., 1952.

Tournier, Paul. *The Meaning of Persons*. New York: Harper and Brothers, 1957.

Pastoral Approach to Old Age and the Problems of Old Age

Arthur, Julietta. *How to Help Older People*. New York: J. B. Lippincott Co., 1954.

The Congregation and the Older Adult. New York: Division of Welfare, Nashville Lutheran Council, 1959.

Doerffler, Alfred. *Treasures of Hope*. St. Louis: Concordia Publishing House, 1945.

Gleason, George. *Horizons for Older People*. New York: The Macmillan Co., 1956.

Jackson, Edgar N. *Understanding Grief*. Nashville: Abingdon Press, 1957.

Man and His Years (First National Conference on Aging). Raleigh, N. C., Health Publications Institute, 1951.

Maves, Paul. *The Best Is Yet to Be*. Philadelphia: The Westminster Press, 1951.

———— and Cedarleaf, J. Lennart. *Older People and the Church*. Nashville: Abingdon Press, 1949.

Index

Escapism, 157
Estrangement, 64-65, 107, 126
Eternal Life, 156-57, 176-77
Eternity, 144, 156
Eustis, Helen, 97
Evangelical Academies, 162
Evangelism, 13, 33, 139, 197
Evangelist, 156
Eve, 119-20
Extrovert-Introvert, 121, 122

Failure, 142, 153, 166
Faith, 33, 43, 67, 70, 85, 101-2, 107,
    118-19, 127, 131, 133, 154-55,
    157, 177
Familism, 9
Family Life Publications, 58
Father, 25, 32, 46, 52, 53, 89-90, 91,
    93, 103, 112, 118, 131, 133, 145,
    165
Father confessor, 50
Fellowship,
    of believers, 63, 66, 87, 129, 132,
    136, 151, 160-61, 181, 186, 195
    of the Church, 63, 161
Femininity, 23, 25, 56
Flesh, 41, 107, 176
Forgiveness, 28, 31-33, 52, 92, 101,
    138
Frakes, Margaret, 190
Freedom, 117, 123
Freud, 35
Frustration, 28, 42, 48, 68, 70, 78-
    79, 95, 97, 105, 107, 113, 143,
    171

Garden of Eden, 119
Geiseman, O. A., 59
Genesis, 16, 22
Geriatrician, 173
Geriatrics problems, 183
Geriatrics worker, 10
Gimmicks, 14
Goals, 142, 154-55
Gospel, 12, 14, 63, 65, 77, 94, 101,
    104, 112, 115, 131, 135, 161,
    163, 167, 186, 194-95
Gospels, 53
Grace, 11, 30, 33, 48, 106, 196
Grandmother, 159

Gratitude, 77, 186
Grief, 170, 187
Group dynamics, 13, 197
Group leader, 136-37
Group work, 196-97
Growth, 106, 112, 145, 177, 193-94
Guidance, 43-45, 70, 109, 163
    postmarital, 60
    premarital, 45-63, 85, 109
Guilt, 28, 36, 44, 65, 70, 94-95, 99,
    108, 111, 113, 117-27, 130-32,
    143, 150, 171, 174
Gumpert, Martin, 173
Gynecologist, 166

Heaven, 170
Heavenly Parent, 94-95, 124
Hebrews, 159
Hebrews, letter to the, 102, 107
Hellenist, 27, 29
Hiltner, Seward, 14
Hines, James, 56, 58
"Hitting bottom," 84, 92
Holy Spirit, 66, 70, 106, 107, 134,
    163, 176-77, 194
Homemaker, 24
Homiletics, 13, 134
Hosea, 17
Hostile, 122, 142
Hostility, 142, 179
Howe, Reuel, 95
Humility, 107, 157-58
Husband, 24-25, 27, 31-34, 42, 52-
    53, 56, 71-87, 145, 149, 152,
    164-65
Husband-wife relationship, 60, 110

Id, 35
Idol, 157, 214
Idolatry, 34, 130
Individualism, 192, 197
Individualization, 119
Indulgence, 109
Inferiority, 80, 121, 133, 152
Infertility pills, 39
Infidelity, 81-83, 152
Initiative, 101, 134, 184
In-law, 52-53, 75, 96
Insecurity, 80, 147
Insight, 57, 113, 137, 197